Henry Webb Brewster

Sensation and Intellection

Their Character and their Function in the Cognition of the Real and the Ideal

Henry Webb Brewster

Sensation and Intellection
Their Character and their Function in the Cognition of the Real and the Ideal

ISBN/EAN: 9783337372071

Printed in Europe, USA, Canada, Australia, Japan

Cover: Foto ©Thomas Meinert / pixelio.de

More available books at **www.hansebooks.com**

Sensation and Intellection

THEIR CHARACTER AND THEIR FUNCTION

IN THE

COGNITION OF THE REAL AND THE IDEAL.

A Thesis,

PRESENTED FOR THE DEGREE OF PH. D. AT THE
UNIVERSITY OF MINNESOTA,

By HENRY WEBB BREWSTER, A. B.

1892.

_____

MINNEAPOLIS:
THE UNIVERSITY OF MINNESOTA,
1893.

"A careful study of the various theories which have been held concerning sensation would be of as much interest and importance as an investigation of any one point in the range of philosophy. In the theory of a philosopher about sensation we have the reflex of his fundamental category and the clew to his further doctrine. Sensation stands on the border-line between the world of nature and the realm of soul; and every advance in science, every development of philosophy, leaves its impress in a charge in the theory of sensation."

Dewey's Leibniz, p. 87.

"Only some form of Monism that shall satisfy the facts and truths to which both Realism and Idealism appeal can occupy the place of true and final philosophy. . . . Some form of Monism which shall incorporate both Realism and Idealism is, therefore, at present, the intelligent and avowed aim of philosophy. The tendency of modern thought toward a form of speculative thinking that is a 'Real-Idealism' or an 'Ideal-Realism,' is unmistakable."

Ladd's Introduction to Philosophy, pp. 407-8.

CONTENTS.

BOOK II.

The ambiguous use of technical terms is a great hindrance to the advance of any science, and psychology seems to suffer more in this respect than any other. Dr. Ward, in his article in the Ency. Brit., puts it none too strongly when he says that "it seems to be the fate of this science to be restricted in its terminology to the ill-defined and well-worn currency of common speech, with which every psychologist feels at liberty to do what seems right in his own eyes, at least within the wide range which a loose connotation allows." In no case is this ambiguity greater or more confusing than in the use of the term sensation. Sensation and intellection are fundamental characteristics of every stage, process, or content of human consciousness; yet the definition of neither can be found clearly stated in psychological literature. The necessity of precise definitions has, of course, been recognized, and repeated attempts have been made to give them; but the definitions have varied with each successive writer, who has generally, since the time of Locke, restricted the scope of the term sensation and broadened that of intellection. In this way the term sensation has been successively narrowed in meaning from Berkeley's sweeping inclusion of "the sun, moon, and stars, and every other object of the senses," down through Hamilton's "subject-object" and J. S. Mill's "signs of Permanent Possibilities," to Herbert Spencer's unconscious "nervous shock," or "ultimate unit of consciousness." And finally, T. H. Green argues that neither sensation nor intellection can have any meaning taken separately; but that, on the contrary, they are "inseparable and mutually dependent," and "each in its full reality includes the other."

The term sensation being still used in many of these different senses, it becomes highly important to determine the number of essentially different views held concerning its nature, and the relation of these views to one another. In analyzing the nature and relation of sensation and intellection, it is necessary to discuss the relation of the relative and the absolute to the ideal and the real; and in setting forth their functions, it is necessary to set forth the distinction between the ideal and the real, in order to show either the correspondence of the primary sub-divisions of each to the fundamental intellectual faculties, or the function of each of these faculties in cognition. Book I. of this thesis gives an analysis of sensation and intellection, defines each, and determines the relation of each to the other and to consciousness as a whole. Book II. discusses the distinction between the ideal and the real, the correspondence of the primary sub-divisions of each to the fundamental intellectual faculties, and the function of sensation and intellection in the cognition of each.

BOOK I.

Analysis of Sensation and Intellection.

PART I.

HISTORICAL REVIEW.

CHAPTER I.

PRELIMINARY OUTLINE.

The attempt to distinguish between intellect and sense grew out of efforts to discover and explain the relation between identity and change. In all efforts to explain change by referring it as an effect to some fixed identity as a cause, there has been a general tendency to refer change as phenomenal, wholly or in part, to an origin in the consciousness of the perceiving subject; and this reference is the basis of most theories regarding the nature of sensation. On the other hand, the fixed identity, which is supposed to be causally related to change, is usually postulated as a substance existing independent of consciousness; and the faculty by which this is cognized is termed intellect, the function of which is intellection. While this association of sense with the perception of change and of intellect with the cognition of identity has formed the basis of all distinctions between sensation and intellection, the real nature of this distinction seems never to have been clearly stated.

Parmenides appears to have been the first to distinguish between reason and sense. He regarded reason as the source of the knowledge of reality, and sense as the source of the illusory appearance of change. Plato further emphasized the distinction made by Parmenides, giving to intellectual cognition the name γνῶσις and to sense-perception the name αἴσθησις. Aristotle restored unity to these divorced aspects of sentience by making them supplementary factors of one process, instead of two conflicting processes. Since Aristotle's time, philosophers have generally overlooked the correlative nature of these two aspects of consciousness, and represented them as two separate activities. By some writers they have been represented as of equal importance; and by others each has been represented as of sole importance. The distinction between intellectual perception and sense-perception, however, has gradually been changed into a distinction between intellect and sense, and this again into a distinction between intellection and sensation. In tracing the history of the distinctions made between these two contrasted terms it will be both easier and clearer to follow in connected sequence the treatment of each separately. It will also be much clearer to trace fully the history of each, before giving a critical analysis of the same, than it would to mingle history and criticism together. In order clearly to set forth the correlative theory of sensation it is necessary first to analyze the nature of intellection, hence the two terms, sensation and intellection, will be treated in an order the reverse of that in which they appear in the title.

The names of the writers most prominently associated with the treatment of intellection are Descartes, Geulincx, Malebranche, Spinoza, Leibniz, Kant, Fichte, Schelling, Hegel, and Herbart; and the treatment of the subject by them in successive order has been that of a continuous development. The treatment of sensation, on the other hand, is marked by the development of three essentially different views. The first theory developed identifies sense-perception, either entirely or in part, with sensation; and hence may appropriately be called the Sensational Theory. It has appeared in three distinct forms. The first form, which identifies sense-perception in its entirety with sensation, was supported by Hobbes, Locke, Berkeley and Hume. The second form, which identified sensation with a sub-division of sense-perception, the perception of so-called subjective percepts, has been supported by many writers, prominent among whom are Reid, Hamilton, J. S. Mill, Lotze, Murray and Sully. The third form, which identifies sensation with the incipient stages of sense-perception, originated with Fichte; but has been recently supported by Ward and James. The second theory developed reduces sensation to the subordinate rank of a component element in sense-perception; and hence may appropriately be called the Component Theory. It has appeared in two distinct forms. The first form, which reduced sensation to the formless matter of sense-perception, originated with Kant and was supported by Reinhold. The second form, which regards sensations as ultimate units of consciousness, separately unconscious, has been supported by many writers, conspicuously by Spencer, Lewes, and Fick. The third theory, the last to be developed, has never been definitely formulated; but as it denies any separate existence to either sensation or intellection and claims that each includes the other, it may appropriately be called the Correlative Theory. It originated with Green, has been more fully developed by Dewey, and is supported by Ladd. Each of these three principal theories will be made the subject of a separate chapter in both the historical review and the critical analysis of sensation.

CHAPTER II.

The Nature of Intellection.

Modern writers, as was stated on p. 7, have shown a general tendency to widen the meaning of the term intellection at the expense of the term sensation, yet different theories of the former, corresponding to those of the latter, have not appeared. In fact, intellection seems never to have been precisely defined by psychologists. It has been alluded to, on p. 11, as the funcion of the intellect; but just what this function is, can best be shown after both intellection and sensation have been analyzed, since the distinction between the two enters into the definition of each. In general, however, intellection may be said to include the fundamental principles of finite knowledge, the primary laws resting upon them, and the universal processes of thought governed by these laws. The disclosure of these principles, laws and processes has progressed from the particular to the general; and hence it will be easier to analyze and define them in their historical order.

Socrates led the way in the discovery that universal processes of thought dominate every individual consciousness in every field of thought. Before his time such processes had been recognized in the subject of mathematics, but he disclosed their presence also in the defining of concepts and in the field of morals.

Plato made the first attempt to systematize universal processes of thought, and to set forth their relations to objects of sense. But inasmuch as he regarded change as belonging to the individual objects of sense-perception, he held all universals to be unchangeable entities existing independent of consciousness; and hence his system of ideas, although each was supposed to sustain a generic relation to a multitude of sensible objects, were indefinable and incapable either of enumeration or of classification among themselves. Had Plato understood the nature of his problem, had he realized that he was dealing with universal processes of thought instead of unchangeable things, he doubtless would have perceived that the universal aspect of consciousness, or intellect, could have no meaning or existence except in connection with the variable aspect, or sense. But failing to perceive this, he discarded sense-perception as deceptive; and thus reduced universal processes of thought to mere abstractions, and rendered the classification of sense-objects meaningless.

ARISTOTLE again restored unity to consciousness by uniting the functions of sense and intellect in every activity of thought. This enabled him to systematize a classification of generic and specific names for objects of sense and to adapt this classification to the variable inductions of individual experience.

Another advance which he made upon Plato was his definite enumeration of the categories, or universal processes of thought. And his distinct recognition, in opposition to Plato, of the validity of the data of sense-perception, further showed itself in the fact that his list of categories, viz., substance, quantity, quality, relation, where, when, action, passion and possession, includes several in which the sensational element is prominent.

A third and most important advance made by Aristotle was the formulation of the law of identity and contradiction. From the fact that his system of classification was perfectly adapted both to sense-objects and to the quantitative relations of pure-mathematics, and from the further fact that the law of identity and contradiction applied equally to both, Aristotle failed to distinguish between empirical and a priori judgments. This necessarily led him somewhat astray in regard to both. His treatment of a judgment as the inclusion of a minor term in a major does not strictly apply to inductions of experience; and, on the other hand, the law of identity and contradiction applies to *a priori* judgments only when they express mathematical relations.

DESCARTES, in modern times, took a more advanced position, when he made the conscious ego the basis of all certitude in thought. This makes the conscious self a correlate of every object of thought; yet Descartes so far failed to see this that he set up an antithesis of spirit and matter, making thought an attribute of spirit, and extension an attribute of matter independent of thought. From Descartes' classification of ideas into *fictæ*, *adventitiæ*, and *innatiæ*, the theory of innate ideas originated; and in this theory the categories assumed the character of innate ideas.

GEULINCX, in his doctrine of occasionalism, caught obscurely an important principle, which is an advance upon Aristotle's reference of all phenomena to an origin in an unmoved cause of motion. This advance consisted in making human consciousness an intermediate ·agency between infinite consciousness and the origin of phenomena. Geulincx, however, reversed the true logical order by representing human consciousness as the originating source, and infinite consciousness as the medium of expression.

MALEBRANCHE corrects this position in two respects. He made human consciousness intermediate between infinite consciousness and phenomena, and he also represented the manifestations of conscious activity as governed by fixed laws instead of by occasional impulses.

SPINOZA showed by his method of reasoning from the finite to the infinite that he consciously transcended the law of identity and contradiction, and grasped the principles underlying two other primary laws of thought, one governing the use of strict correlatives, and the other restricting the application of categories when they come into mutual conflict. His conception of the infinite was incompatible with his conception of an efficient cause, for the latter implied and the former precluded temporal limitations. Spinoza therefore discarded the category of causality, and reasoned to the infinite from the finite through the principle of correlativity. Had he, however, comprehended the nature of this correlation, as affected by Descartes' reference of all objects of thought to the conscious ego as a correlate, he never would have made thought an attribute of substance, but would have made substance a category of thought.

LEIBNIZ did philosophy a great service by counteracting the pantheistic tendency which Spinoza's doctrine of substance had given it. Having rejected Spinoza's conclusion, Leibniz naturally rejected his method of reasoning also; but feeling the inadequacy of the principle of causality, he sought a better one in what he termed the "principle of sufficient reason," "*principium rationis sufficientis.*" This principle has never been defined otherwise than as "necessity in thought;" but as necessity in thought comes only through the law of identity or the law of correlation, it must come under one of these laws. As the principle of sufficient reason is usually employed, it is the same as that of correlativity. Leibniz' monadology, although full of inconsistencies, has done much to maintain the view that finite consciousness is characterized by individuality and spontaneity.

Contemporaneous with this last group of writers, to whom we are greatly indebted for the elucidation of the principles of intellection, was a class of sensational writers, whose work, even though it held to the principle "*Nihil est in intellectu quod non ante fuerit in sensu,*" greatly helped to bring to the front the laws and principles of intellection. Thus, Locke really rendered an important service to the intellectualists by his polemic against innate ideas. Hume's challenge concerning the principle of causality but forced them to a new and an important advance. From the sensational standpoint, the category of causality must either come through the senses or be an illusory fiction; yet Hume proved that it could not come through the senses. The intellectualists then had to give a satisfactory account of it, or surrender it as illusory. To surrender it was to surrender all claim to either science or philosophy. Hume's challenge met a master intellect in Kant, who not only gave a satisfactory account of the origin of the category of causality, but also disclosed the fundamental fallacies of sensationalism.

KANT successfully terminated the long-continued effort to discover the origin of necessary ideas, by showing that they are the product of universal processes of thought. Profiting by Locke's polemic against innate ideas, he states that "they admit, if separated from sensibility, of no use at all; that is, they cannot be applied to any possible object, and are nothing but the pure form of the use of the understanding with reference to objects in general."[1] In answer to Hume's sensationalism, he shows that all experience must be organically related to a "unity of apperception;" and that this organic unification requires, possesses, and discloses universal and invariable processes of thought. These universal processes of thought are the categories, with the use of which he connected "the concept, or, if the term be preferred, the judgment, 'I think,'" which he styled "the vehicle of all concepts in general."[2] That Kant failed, however, to perceive the correlative nature of the categories is shown by his agreement with Aristotle on the application of the law of contradiction, by his first two groups of categories, and by his antinomies of pure reason. But that he perceived the necessity for some limitation of the categories when they came into mutual conflict, is shown by his doctrine of phenomena and noumena.

FICHTE brought to attention the correlative nature of the universal processes of thought by showing that a category is a synthesis of two correlative opposites, and that each correlate included as well as excluded the other. He failed, however, to perceive the full force of the correlative principle, and represented a pair of correlates as inclusive only in part and as exclusive only in so far as they were not inclusive. This is shown in his treatment of

---

1 "Critique of Pure Reason," Max Mueller's Translation, p. 216.
2 id. p. 297.

limitation. Instead of reconciling the ego and the non-ego in a correlative unity, he reduced the non-ego to a mere limitation of the ego; and since Kant had disclosed the universal aspect of all processes of thought, Fichte sublated the non-ego in the ego, and the individuality of the ego in its universality, and so ended with a universal pantheism of an idealistic nature.

He thus confused the principle of correlativity, which underlies the law of correlation, with the principle of relativity, which underlies the law of contradiction. In accordance with the law of contradiction, all sense objects and all quantitative terms of pure mathematics can be classified into genera and species, each genus *including* several mutually *excluding* species. But neither the *inclusion* nor the *exclusion* of a pair of correlates under the law of correlation is of this quantitative nature. This can be illustrated by means of a line drawn, for instance, north and south. In accordance with the law of contradiction, the two ends may be said each to include half of the line, and both to mutually exclude each other. In accordance with the law of correlation, however, neither the inclusion nor the exclusion has a quantitative significance; but the mutually including and excluding terms are simply opposed aspects of a unity, which is quantitatively indivisible in so far as it is characterized by these terms. Thus, if the north half of the line were erased there would still remain a line with both a north end and a south end; and if the erasing were continued, this would remain true until the line wholly disappeared, when the correlative aspects would vanish together. Applying this illustration to the relation of the ego and the non-ego; it will be seen that the two are, not quantitative divisions, but correlative aspects of finite consciousness; and that while each, from a separate point of view, excludes the other, both are mutually dependent and inseparable aspects of an indivisible unity.

SCHELLING, realizing Fichte's failure correctly to set forth the principle of correlativity, attempted to remedy the error by reducing the opposition between correlative opposites to a complete indifference. But his total indifference of subject and object, which received the name of "System of Identity," instead of explaining the principle of correlativity, annihilated it.

HEGEL set forth the principle of correlativity in its true nature, except that, instead of representing each category as a unity of two correlates, he included a transitional mean between them, and thus grouped his categories in threes. In applying the principle of correlativity to his doctrine of the absolute, Hegel very naturally carried it too far, and held "that the Absolute, or Reason, is the unity of subjectivity and objectivity;"[1] also "that the common consciousness can demand that a ladder be furnished it upon which it can ascend to the absolute standpoint."[2] These statements violate the law of thought which governs the use of categories when they come into mutual conflict, as they do when applied to the infinite. Finite reason may properly be called the "unity of subjectivity and objectivity"; but absolute reason transcends such qualifications, except as they refer, not to the infinite in itself, but merely to the aspects which it assumes in finite cognition. Again, while "the common consciousness can" comprehend the correlative relation of the finite to the infinite, it never "can ascend to the absolute standpoint."

HERBART perceived the nature of this law governing the mutual conflict of categories, and also Hegel's violation of it; but instead of formulating the law and defining the principle on which it rests, he merely indicated its nature by referring to all conflicting aspects of the infinite as "accidental views" (Erdmann), or "contingent aspects" (Schwegler). Had Herbart accepted Hegel's principle of correlativity and modified his doctrine of "accidental views" accordingly, he might have made a great advance; but in rejecting the principle of correlativity and in applying the law of contradiction to all processes of

---

1 Erdmann's His. of Phil., Vol. II, p. 687.

2 id. p. 684.

thought, he reduced his doctrine of "reals" to a play upon abstractions.

A summary of the analysis of intellection gives two fundamental principles determining the character of finite knowledge, and three primary laws governing the processes of thought. The principle first disclosed is that of *relativity*, which has taken two distinct forms underlying two corresponding laws of thought, the law of *contradiction*, which was formulated by Aristotle, and the law of *mutual limitation*, which was developed by Herbart but not formulated by him. The second principle is that of *correlativity*, underlying the law of *correlation*. This principle was disclosed by Fichte and developed by Hegel, but the law resting upon it has never been formulated. The deduction and definition of the universal processes of thought can best be given in the critical analysis of intellection, after various attempts at their deduction have been criticised; also, the further definition of the fundamental principles of knowledge and the corresponding primary laws of thought can best be given after the categories have been defined and classified.

CHAPTER III.

§1. *Sensation as Sense-Perception.*—This view originated with Hobbes, was formulated by Locke, and was supported by Berkeley and Hume. Hume, however, restricted the definition of sensation slightly, and so led the way to the second form of this theory.

HOBBES defines sense as follows:—"Concerning the thoughts of man, I will consider them first *singly*, and afterwards in *train*, or dependence upon one another. *Singly*, they are everyone a *representative* or *appearance*, of some quality, or other accident of a body without us; which is commonly called an *object*. Which object worketh on the eyes, ears, and other parts of man's body; and by diversity of workings, produceth diversity of appearances. * * * The original of them all, is that which we call *sense* (For there is no conception in man's mind, which hath not at first, totally, or by parts, been begotten upon the organs of sense.); the rest are derived from that original. * * * The cause of sense, is the external body, or object, which presseth the organ proper to each sense, either immediately, as in taste and touch; or mediately, as in seeing, hearing, and smelling; which pressure, by the mediation of nerves, and other strings, and membranes of the body, continued inwards to the brain, and heart, causeth there a resistence, or counter-pressure, or endeavour of the heart to deliver itself; which endeavour, because *outward*, seemeth to be some matter without. And this *seeming*, or *fancy*, is that which men call sense. * * * But when we would express the *decay*, and signify that the sense is fading, old, and past, it is called *memory.*

So that *imagination* and *memory*, are but one thing, which for divers considerations hath divers names."[1]

LOCKE defines sensation, and distinguishes between it and reflection, as follows:—"First, our senses, conversant about particular sensible objects, do *convey into the mind* several distinct *perceptions* of things, according to those various ways wherein those objects do affect them. And thus we come by those *ideas* we have of yellow, white, heat, cold, soft, hard, bitter, sweet, and all those which we call sensible qualities; which when I say the senses convey into the mind, I mean, they from external objects convey into the mind what produces there those *perceptions.* This great source of most of the *ideas* we have, depending wholly upon our senses, and derived by them to the understanding, I call *sensation.* * * * Secondly, the other fountain, from which experience furnisheth the understanding with *ideas,* is the *perception of the operations of our own minds* within us, as it is employed about the *ideas* it has got ;which operations, when the soul comes to reflect on and consider, do furnish the understanding with another set of *ideas,* which could not be had from things without; and such are *perception, thinking, doubting, believing, reasoning, knowing, willing,* and all the different actings of our own minds; which we being conscious of, and observing in ourselves, do from these receive into our understanding as distinct ideas, as we do from bodies affecting our senses. This source of *ideas* every man has wholly in himself; and though it be not sense, as having nothing to do with external objects, yet is very like it, and might properly enough be called internal sense. But as I call the other *sensation,* so I call this *reflection,* the *ideas* it affords being such only as the the mind gets by reflecting on its own operations within itself."[2]

BERKELEY agreed with Locke in identifying sensation with sense-perception; but he tried, by representing sensation as an active function of the mind, to avoid the absurdity of representing extended objects as being im-

1 "The Leviathan." Part I, Chapters I and II.

2 "Essay Concerning Human Understanding." Book II, Chap. I, §§ 3 and 4.

pressed upon the non-extended mind in sense-perception. His great mistake consisted in overlooking the distinction between the individual variability of sensation and the universal invariability of intellection. Berkeley reduced all knowledge to a sensational basis, and thus virtually committed philosophy to the scepticism disclosed by Hume. Berkeley's views are clearly expressed in the following quotations: "Did men but consider that the sun, moon, and stars, and every other object of the senses, are only so many sensations in their minds, which have no other existence but barely being perceived, doubtless they would never fall down and worship their own *ideas;* but rather address their homage to that *eternal invisible Mind* which produces and sustains all things."[1] "In short, let any one consider those arguments, which are thought manifestly to prove that colours and tastes exist only in the mind, and he shall find they may with equal force, be brought to prove the same thing of extension, figure, and motion."[2]

HUME states this view of sensation in the following words: "All the perceptions of the human mind resolve themselves into two distinct kinds, which I shall call *impressions* and *ideas.* The difference betwixt these consists in the degrees of force and liveliness, with which they strike upon the mind, and make their way into our thought or consciousness. Those perceptions which enter with the most force and violence, we may name *impressions;* and under this name, I comprehend all our sensations, passions and emotions, as they make their first appearance in the soul. By *ideas* I mean the faint images of these in thinking and reasoning; such as, for instance, are all the perceptions excited by the present discourse, excepting only those which arise from the sight and touch, and excepting the immediate pleasure or uneasiness it may occasion."[3] "Impressions may be divided into two kinds, those of *sensation* and those of *reflection.* The

---

1 " Principles of Human Knowledge," Part I., Sec. 94.

2 id. Sec. 15.

3 " Treatise on Human Nature," Green & Grose's Ed. p. 311.

first kind arises in the soul originally, from unknown causes. The second is derived in a great measure from our ideas, and that in the following order. An impression first strikes upon the senses, and makes us perceive heat or cold, thirst or hunger, pleasure or pain of some kind or other. Of this impression there is a copy taken by the mind, which remains after the impression ceases; and this we call an idea. This idea of pleasure or pain, when it returns upon the soul, produces the new impressions of desire and aversion, hope and fear, which may properly be called impressions of reflection, because derived from it."[1] "As to those *impressions*, which arise from the *senses*, their ultimate cause is, in my opinion, perfectly inexplicable by human reason, and 'twill always be impossible to decide with certainty, whether they arise immediately from the object, or are produced by the creative power of the mind, or are derived from the author of our being."[2]

§2. *Sensations as Subjective Affections.*—THOMAS REID originated the view which identifies sensation with sense-perception, when the latter is regarded as a mere affection of the perceiving subject abstracted from all reference to physical causes. The following are his own statements:— "*Sensation* is a name given by philosophers to an act of mind, which may be distinguished from all others by this, that it hath no object distinct from the act itself. Pain of every kind is an uneasy sensation."[3] "Almost all our perceptions have corresponding sensations which constantly accompany them, and, on that account, are very apt to be confounded with them. * * * Hence it happens, that a quality perceived, and the sensation corresponding to that perception, often go under the same name. This makes the names of most of our sensations ambiguous. * * * When I smell a rose, there is in this operation both sensation and perception. The agreeable odor I feel, considered by itself, without relation to any external

---

1 op. cit. pp. 316-7.

2 id. p. 385.

3 "Works of Thomas Reid," Hamilton's Ed., p. 229.

object, is merely a sensation. * * * Observing that the
agreeable sensation is raised when the rose is near, and
ceases when it is removed, I am led by my nature, to conclude some quality to be in the rose, which is the cause of
this sensation. This quality in the rose is the object perceived; and the act of my mind by which I have the con-
viction and belief of this quality, is what in this case I call
perception. * * * But it is here to be observed, that
the sensation I feel, and the quality in the rose which I
perceive, are both called by the same name."[1]

HAMILTON states this view very fully, and illustrates it
with examples. The following quotations set forth his
views:—"In Perception proper there is a higher energy of
intelligence, than in Sensation proper. For though the
latter be the apprehension of an affection of the Ego, and
therefore, in a certain sort, the apprehension of an im-
material quality; still it is only the apprehension of the
fact of an organic passion; whereas the former, though
supposing Sensation as its condition, and though only
the apprehension of the attributes of a material Non-ego,
is, however, itself without corporeal passion, and, at the
same time, the recognition not merely of a fact, but of relations."[2] "Sensation proper has no object but a subject-
object, i. e., the organic affection of which we are conscious. * * * Sensation proper, viewed on one side, is
a passive affection of the organism; but viewed on the
other, it is an active apperception, by the mind, of that
affection."[3] "Aristotle's discrimination of the Common
and Proper Sensibles or Percepts embodies not only the
modern distinction of the Primary and Secondary Qualities of matter, but also the modern distinction of the two
perceptions, Perception proper and Sensation proper."[4]
"Sensation proper and Perception proper were, however,
even more strongly contra-distinguished in the system of

---

1 op. cit. p. 310.
2 O. W. Wight's "Philosophy of Sir William Hamilton," p. 419.
3 id. pp. 421-2.
4 id. p. 433.

the lower Platonists."[1] "In the Cartesian philosophy, the distinction was virtually taken by Descartes, but first discriminated in terms by his followers."[2]

J. S. MILL still further restricts the scope of the term sensation, as is shown by the following quotations:—"The thread of consciousness which I apprehend the sensation as a part of, is the *subject* of the sensation. The group of Permanent Possibilities of Sensation to which I refer it, and which is partially realized and actualized in it, is the *object* of the sensation. * * * We have no conception of either Subject or Object, either Mind or Matter, except as something to which we refer our sensations, and whatever other feelings we are conscious of. The very existence of them both, so far as cognizable by us, consists only in the relation they respectively bear to our states of feeling. Their relation to each other is only the relation between those two relations. The immediate correlatives are not the pair, Object, Subject, but the two pairs, Object, Sensation objectively considered; Subject, Sensation subjectively considered. * * * The difference between these two classes of our sensations, answers to the distinction made by a majority of philosophers between the Primary and the Secondary Qualities of Matter. * * * There are, however, some of our sensations, in our consciousness of which the reference to their Object does not play so conspicuous and predominant a part as in others. This is particularly the case with sensations which are highly interesting to us on their own account, and on which we willingly dwell, or which by their intensity compel us to concentrate our attention on them. These are, of course, our pleasures and pains. * * * Those of our sensations, on the contrary, which are almost indifferent in themselves, our attention does not dwell on; our consciousness of them is too momentary to be distinct, and we pass on from them to the Permanent Possibilities of Sensation which they are the signs of, and which are alone of importance to us. We hardly notice

1 op. cit. p. 434.
2 id. p. 435.

the relation between these sensations and the subjective chain of consciousness of which they form so extremely insignificant a part, the sensation is hardly anything to us but the link which draws into consciousness a group of Permant Possibilities; this group is the only thing distinctly present to our thoughts."[1]

LOTZE unites in sensations the characteristics assigned to them by both Hamilton and Mill. In his theory of "Local Signs" he asserts the existence of separate, non-spatial sensations in the soul, each of which has "a certain accessory impression" which acts as a sign to determine its spatial relations. His own statements are as follows:— "Many impressions exist conjointly in the soul, although not spatially side by side with one another; but they are merely together in the same way as the synchronous tones of a chord; that is to say, qualitatively different, but not side by side with, above or below, one another. Notwithstanding, the mental presentation of a spatial order must be produced again from these impressions. The question is, therefore, in the first place, to be raised: How in general does the soul come to apprehend these impressions, not in the form in which they actually are—to-wit, non-spatial,—but as they are not, in a spatial juxtaposition? * * * Accordingly we conceive of this in the following way: Every impression of color r—for example, red— produces on all places of the retina, which it reaches, the same sensation of redness. In addition to this, however, it produces on each of these different places, a, b, c, a certain accessory impression, α, β, γ, which is independent of the nature of the color seen, and dependent merely on the nature of the place excited. This second local impression would therefore be associated with every impression of color r, in such manner that r α signifies a red that acts upon the point a, r β signifies the same red in case it acts upon the point b. These associated accessory impressions would, accordingly, render for the soul the clue, by following which it transposes the same red, now to one, now to another spot, or simultaneously to different spots in the space intuited by it."[1]

MURRAY makes sensations "elementary facts of mind" that cannot be defined, yet that can be consciously felt and distinguished. The following is his own statement: "For sensations, being the simple elementary facts of mind, cannot be defined or described by anything more simple or elementary. The only way in which a sensation can be known is by being *felt*."[2]

SULLY agrees with Murray that a sensation is an "elementary mental phenomenon" indefinable as it appears in consciousness, but definable as related to the physical conditions involved in its stimulation. He says: "A sensation being an elementary mental phenomenon cannot be defined in terms of anything more simple. Its meaning can only be indicated by a reference to the nervous process on which it is known to depend. Accordingly a sensation may be defined as a simple mental state resulting from the stimulation of the outer extremity of an incarrying nerve, when this stimulation has been transmitted to the brain centers."[3]

§ 3. *Sensation as Incipient Sense-Perception.*—FICHTE originated this view of sensation, and, according to the following quotation from Erdmann, makes sensation an incipient stage of sense-perception: "Fichte has often confessed his 'boundless' respect for Maimon's genius, which gave the first impulse towards his theory of sensation."[4] "The development begins with the very lowest step of that unconscious act of creation, that state in which intelligence first *discovers* what is already, it is true, *in itself*, viz., *sensation*. This is taken as the state in which no distinction is as yet made between external and internal sensation, and just as little between that which feels sensation and that which is felt as such. Inasmuch as the (centrifugal) ego transcends sensation, it dis-

---

1 "Outlines of Psychology," Ladd's Translation, pp. 50-3.

2 "Hand-book of Psychology," p. 30.

3 " Teachers' Hand-Book of Psychology," p. 86.

4 " History of Philosophy," vol ii, p, 483.

tinguishes itself from it, and the latter thereby acquires a reference to something beyond itself."[1]

DR. WARD identifies sensation with an incipient stage of presentation, in which "we are able to distinguish the conscious subject and the 'affection' of which it is conscious." He also assigns to sensation "two 'aspects,' the one a 'sensible or intellectual' or 'qualitative,' the other an 'affective' or 'emotive.'" His own statements are as follows: "The ordinary conception of a sensation coincides, no doubt, with the definition given by Hamilton and Mansel: 'Sensation proper is the consciousness of certain affections of our body as an animated organism;' and it is because in ordinary thinking we reckon the body as a part of self that we come to think of sensations as subjective modifications. But when considerations of method compel us to eliminate physiological implications from the ordinary conception of a sensation, we are able here to distinguish the conscious subject and the 'affections' of which it is conscious, as clearly as we can distinguish subject and object in other cases of presentation. * * * * Thus the further we go back the nearer we approach to a total presentation having the character of one general *continuum* in which differences are latent, * * * a certain objective continuum forming the background or basis to the several relatively distinct presentations that are elaborated out of it."[2] "Accordingly all the more recent psychologists have been driven by one means or another to recognize two 'aspects' (Bain), or 'properties' (Wundt), in what they call a sensation, the one a 'sensible or intellectual' or 'qualitative,' the other an 'affective' or 'emotive;' aspect or property."[3]

PROF. JAMES gives the latest, fullest and most definite account of this view, as the following quotations will show: "*Sensation, then, so long as we take the analytic point of view, differs from Perception only in the extreme*

1 op. cit. p. 503.
2 Ency. Brit., vol. xx., pp. 41-2.
3 id. p. 40.

simplicity of its object or content."[1] "Some persons will
say that we never have a really simple object or content.
My definition of sensation does not require the simplicity
to be absolutely, but only relatively, extreme."[2] "As we
can only think or talk about the relations of objects with
which we have *acquaintance* already, we are forced to
postulate a function in our thought whereby we first become aware of the *bare immediate natures* by which our
several objects are distinguished. This function is sensation."[3] "Sensations are the stable rock, the *terminus a
quo* and the *terminus ad quem* of thought. To find such
termini is our aim with all our theories—to conceive first
when and where a certain sensation may be had, and then
to have it. Finding it, stops discussion. Failure to find
it kills the false conceit of knowledge. * * * *Pure sensations can only be realized in the earliest days of life.*
They are all but impossible to adults with memories and
stores of associations acquired. Prior to all impressions
on sense-organs the brain is plunged in deep sleep and consciousness is practically non-existent. Even the first
weeks after birth are passed in almost unbroken sleep by
human infants. It takes a strong message from the sense-
organs to break this slumber. In a new born brain this
gives rise to an absolutely pure sensation. * * * *The
first sensation which an infant gets is for him the universe.*
And the universe which he later comes to know is nothing
but an amplification and an implication of that first
simple germ which, by accretion on the one hand and in-
tussusception on the other, has grown so big and complex and articulate that its first estate is unrememberable.
In his dumb awakening to the consciousness of *something
there*, a mere *this* as yet (or something for which even the
term *this* would perhaps be too discriminative, and the
intellectual. acknowledgement of which would be better
expressed by the bare interjection 'lo!'), the infant en-
counters an object in which (though it be given in a pure

1 "Principles of Psychology," vol. ii., pp. 1–2.
2 id. p. 2, foot-note.
3 id. p. 3.

sensation) all the 'categories of the understanding' are contained. It has *objectivity, unity, substantiality, causality, in the full sense in which any later object or system of objects has these things.*"[1]

---

1 op. cit. pp. 7-8.

CHAPTER IV.

THE COMPONENT THEORY OF SENSATION.

§1. *Sensation as Formless Matter.*—KANT's ideas, in which this view of sensation originated, are fairly set forth in the following quotations:—"Our knowledge springs from two fundamental sources of our soul; the first receives representations (receptivity of impressions), the second is the power of knowing an object by these representations (spontaneity of concepts). By the first an object is *given* us, by the second the object is *thought*, in relation to that representation which is a mere determination of the soul. * * * We call *sensibility* the *receptivity* of our soul, or its power of receiving representations whenever it is in any wise affected, while the *understanding*, on the contrary, is with us the power of producing representations, or the *spontaneity* of knowledge."[1] "Both are either pure or empirical. They are empirical when sensation, presupposing the actual presence of the object, is contained in it. They are pure when no sensation is mixed up with the representation. The latter may be called the material of sensuous knowledge."[2] "In a phenomenon I call that which corresponds to the sensation its *matter*; but that which causes the manifold matter of the phenomenon to be perceived as arranged in a certain order, I call its *form*. Now it is clear that it cannot be sensation again through which sensations are arranged and placed in certain forms. The matter only of all phenomena is given us *a posteriori*; but their form must be ready for them in the mind *a priori*, and must therefore be capable of being considered as separate from

---

1 "Critique of Pure Reason," Max Mueller's Translation, pp. 44-5.
d. p. 44.

all sensations. I call all representations in which there is
nothing that belongs to sensation, *pure* (in a transcendental sense). The pure form therefore of all sensuous in-
tuitions, that form in which the manifold elements of the
phenomenon are seen in a certain order, must be found
in the mind *a priori.* And this pure form of sensibility may be called the pure intuition. * * *
In the course of this investigation it will appear that
there are, as principles of *a priori* knowledge, two pure
forms of sensuous intuition, namely, *Space* and *Time.*"¹
"It cannot be denied that phenomena may be given in intuition without the functions of the understanding. * *
* * For we could quite well imagine that phenomena
might possibly be such that the understanding should not
find them conforming to the conditions of its synthetical
unity, and all might be in such confusion that nothing
should appear in the succession of phenomena which
could supply a rule of synthesis, and correspond, for instance, to the concept of cause and effect, so that this concept would thus be quite empty, null and meaningless.
With all this, phenomena would offer objects to our intuition, because intuition by itself does not require the functions of thought."²

REINHOLD supports Kant's theory of sensation, as the
following quotation from Erdmann's "History of Philosophy" will show:—"On account of the double relation in
which, according to the highest principle, the presentation
stands, it must contain two component parts or moments,
the matter corresponding to the presented thing or the
object, and the form corresponding to the presenting subject. * * * If now we reason back to the inner ground
of the presentation, we must distinguish in the faculty of
presentations a faculty for the given, the matter, that is
to say, receptivity, and likewise one for producing the
form, that is to say, spontaniety."³

§2. *Sensations as Ultimate Units of Consciousness.*—

1 op. cit. pp. 18-20.
2 id. pp. 80-1.
3 Vol. II, pp. 476-7.

HERBERT SPENCER states this view at length, and illustrates it by referring to conscious phenomena which he holds to be composed of unconscious infinitessimal units. The following are his own statements:—"Well known experiments prove that when equal blows or taps are made one after another at a rate not exceeding some sixteen per second, the effect of each is perceived as a separate noise; but when the rapidity with which the blows follow one another exceeds this, the noises are no longer identified as separate states of consciousness, and there arises in place of them a continuous state of consciousness, called a tone. On further increasing the rapidity of the blows, the tone undergoes the change of quality distinguished as rise in pitch; and it continues to rise in pitch as the blows continue to increase in rapidity, until it reaches an acuteness beyond which it is no longer appreciable as a tone. So that out of units of feeling of the same kind, many feelings distinguishable from one another in quality result, according as the units are more or less integrated. * * * If the unlikenesses among the sensations of each class may be due to unlikenesses among the modes of aggregation of a unit of consciousness common to them all; so, too, may the much greater unlikenesses between the sensations of each class and those of other classes. There may be a single primordial element of consciousness, and the countless kinds of consciousness may be produced by the compounding of this element with itself and the recompounding of its compounds with one another in higher and higher degrees: so producing increased multiplicity, variety, and complexity. Have we any clue to this primordial element? I think we have. * * * The subjective effect produced by a crack or noise that has no appreciable duration, is little else than a nervous shock. Though we distinguish such a nervous shock as belonging to what we call sounds, yet it does not differ very much from nervous shocks of other kinds. An electric discharge sent through the body, causes a feeling akin to that which a sudden loud report causes. A strong unexpected impression made through the eyes, as by a flash of lightning,

similarly gives rise to a start or shock. * * * The
fact that sudden brief disturbances thus set up by different
stimuli through different sets of nerves, cause feelings
scarcely distinguishable in quality, will not appear strange
when we recollect that distinguishableness of feeling implies appreciable duration; and that when the duration
is greatly abridged, nothing more is known than that
some mental change has occurred and ceased. * * *
It is possible then—may we not even say, probable—that
something of the same order as that which we call a nervous shock is the ultimate unit of consciousness; and that
all the unlikenesses among our feelings result from unlike
modes of integration of this ultimate unit."[1]

FICK supports this theory of unconscious psychic units
and the production of different conscious states from
the same unit differently compounded, and claims that the
theory is proved by the production of feelings of touch
and feelings of temperature from the same unit differently
compounded. He is quoted by Prof. James as follows:
"A feeling of temperature arises when the intensities of
the units of feeling are evenly gradated, so that between
two elements a and b no other unit can spatially inter-
vene whose intensity is not also *between* that of a and b.
A feeling of contact perhaps arises when this condition is
not fulfilled. Both kinds of feeling, however, are composed of the same units."[2] " His own words are: ' Mistakes are made in the sense that he admits having been
touched, when in reality it was radiant heat that affected
his skin. In our own before-mentioned experiments there
was never any deception on the entire palmar side of the
hand or on the face. On the back of the hand in one case
in a series of 60 stimulations 4 mistakes occurred, in another case 2 mistakes in 45 stimulations. On the extensor
side of the upper arm 3 deceptions out of 48 stimulations
were noticed, and in the case of another individual, 1 out
of 31. In one case over the spine 3 deceptions in a series
of 11 excitations were observed; in another, 4 out of 19.

1 **"Principles of Psychology,"** pp. 149-51.
2 " Principles of Psychology," vol. i., p. 151.

On the lumbar spine 6 deceptions came among 29 stimulations, and again 4 out of 7."[1]

G. H. LEWES defends this theory of ultimate units and carries it back to what he calls "the raw material of consciousness," "neural units," "tremors of the psychoplasm." He says:—"If, instead of considering the whole vital organism, we consider solely its sensitive aspects, and confine ourselves to the Nervous System, we may represent the molecular movements of the Bioplasm by the neural tremors of the Psychoplasm; these tremors are what I term *neural units*; the raw material of Consciousness. * * * The movements of the Bioplasm constitute Vitality; the movements of the Psychoplasm constitute Sensibility. * * * Viewing the internal factors solely in the light of Feeling, we may say that the *sentient material* out of which all the forms of Consciousness are evolved is the Psychoplasm incessantly fluctuating, incessantly renewed."[2]

---

1 op. cit. p. 150.
2 "Problems of Life and Mind," Vol. I, pp. 109-10.

CHAPTER V.

T. H. GREEN may justly be called the author of this view. His clearest statements upon the subject are the following:—"In reflecting on the process by which we have come to know anything, we find that, at any stage we may recall, it consists in a further qualification of a given material by the consideration of the material under relations hitherto unconsidered. Thus as contrasted with, and abstracted from, the further formation which upon continued observation and attention it may require, any perception, any piece of knowledge, may be regarded as an unformed matter. On the other hand, when we look at what the given perception or piece of knowledge is in itself, we find that it is already formed, in more complex ways than we can disentangle, by the synthesis of less determinate data. But there is a point at which the individual's retrospective analysis of the knowledge he finds himself to possess necessarily stops. Antecedently to any of the intellectual formative processes which he can trace, it would seem that something must have been given for those processes to begin upon. This something is taken to be feeling, pure and simple. When all accretions of form, due to the intellectual establishment of relations, have been stripped off, there seem to remain the mere sensations without which the intellectual activity would have had nothing to deal with or operate upon. These then must be in an absolute sense the matter—the matter excluding all form—of experience. Now it is evident that the ground on which we make this statement, that mere sensations form the matter of experience, warrants us in making it, if at all, only as a statement in regard to the

mental history of the individual. Even in this reference it
can scarcely be accepted. There is no positive basis for it
but the fact that, so far as memory goes, we always find
ourselves manipulating some data of consciousness, themselves independent of any intellectual manipulation which
we can remember applying to them. But on the strength
of this to assume that there are such data in the history of
our experience, consisting in mere sensations, antecedently
to any action of the intellect, is not really an intelligible
inference from the fact stated. It is an abstraction which
may be put into words, but to which no real meaning can
be attached. For a sensation can only form an object of
experience in being determined by an intelligent subject
which distinguishes it from itself and contemplates it in
relation to other sensations; so that to suppose a primary
datum or matter of the individual's experience, wholly
void of intellectual determination, is to suppose such experience to begin with what could not belong to or be an
object of experience at all. * * * Thus, when we in-
quire whether there is such a thing in the world of phenomena as sensation undetermined by thought, the question
may be considered in relation either to the facts, as such,
or to the consciousness for which the facts exist. It may
be put either thus—Among the facts that form the objects
of possible experience, are there sensations which do not
depend on thought for being what they are? or thus—Is
sensation, as unqualified by thought, an element in the
consciousness which is necessary to there being such a
thing as a world of phenomena? After what has already
been said, the answer to these questions need not detain
us long. If it is admitted that we know of no other medium but a thinking or self-distinguishing consciousness, in
and through which that unification of the manifold can
take place which is necessary to constitute relation, it follows that a sensation apart from thought—not determined or acted upon by thought—would be an unrelated
sensation; and an unrelated sensation cannot amount to a
fact. Mere sensation is in truth a phrase that represents
no reality. It is the result of a process of abstraction;

but having got the phrase we give a confused meaning to it, we fill up the shell which our abstraction has left, by reintroducing the qualification we assumed ourselves to have got rid of. * * * Feeling and thought are inseparable and mutually dependent in the consciousness for which the world of experience exists, inseparable and mutually dependent in the constitution of the facts which form the object of that consciousness. Each in its full reality includes the other. * * * Neither is the product of the other. It is only when by a process of abstraction we have reduced either to something which is not itself, that we can treat either as the product of anything, or apply the category of cause and effect to it at all. For that category is itself their product. Or rather, it represents one form of the activity of the consciousness which in inseparable union they constitute."[1]

DR. DEWEY supports this view and formulates it more definitely than T. H. GREEN, as appears from the following:—"We have now seen that will, knowledge, and feeling are not three kinds of consciousness, but three aspects of the same consciousness. We have also seen that each of these aspects is the result of an artificial analysis, since, in any concrete case, each presupposes the other, and can not exist without it. The necessity of this mutual connection may be realized by reverting to our definition of psychology, where it was said that psychology is the science of the reproduction of some universal content in the form of individual consciousness. Every consciousness, in other words, is the relation of a universal and an individual element, and cannot be understood without both. It will now be evident that the universal element is knowledge, the individual is feeling, while the relation which connects them into one concrete content is will. It will also be seen that knowledge and feeling are partial aspects of the self, and hence more or less abstract, while will is complete, comprehending both aspects."[2] "The sensation is not a fact immediately present in consciousness. We do not have

1 "Prolegomena to Ethics," §§43-50.
2 "Psychology," pp. 20-1.

direct knowledge of it any more than we do of the atom or molecule. Actual mental life is concrete, not made up of isolated atomic sensations. It is thoroughly complex, and no simple element can be immediately laid hold of. In fact, knowledge always consists in *relation* —in the connection of elements, and their mutual reference to each other—and so no isolated, unrelated sensation, such as we suppose forms the material of knowledge, could possibly be immediately known. Sensations are known, then, only as the result of a process of abstraction and analysis, and their existence is supposed only because, without them, it would be impossible to account for the complex phenomena which are directly present in consciousness."[1]

PROF. LADD's treatment of sensation explicitly rejects the first and second theories, and, while it does not state any exact distinction between sensation and intellection, it is, so far as his analysis is carried, in complete harmony with the correlative theory. His position is fairly represented by the following quotations:—"It is essential, in the first place, to distinguish 'simple sensations' from 'presentations of sense,' or those complex objects of consciousness which result from an act of mental synthesis on the basis of several simultaneous affections of sense. As respects developed experience, the *simple* sensation is a necessary fiction of psycho-physical science. Consciousness is scarcely more able directly to analyze a presentation of sense into those factors out of which it originated than it is to analyze a drop of water into its component oxygen and hydrogen gasses."[2] "There are no *sensations* (whatever physical occasions of sensations may exist) except those that appear in consciousness."[3] "It analyzes what is relatively very complex into what is relatively simple and elementary; and it points out the conditions under which, and the terms—so to speak—on which the latter combines into the former. Of course, in doing this

---

1 op. cit. p. 34.

2 "Elements of Physiological Psychology," pp. 305-6.

3 id. p. 362.

the psychologist must not be deceived into supposing that these factors, or 'moments' of psychic life, are entities, after the fashion of the atom or molecule, dealt with by the natural sciences of chemistry and molecular physics. But they are entities in the sense in which psychic facts are entities. The existence of some of them can be readily detected by such analysis as self-consciousness can make; while others of them are rather speculative necessities postulated in the effort to account for the varying characteristics of those complex phenomena which constitute the primary problems of psychology."[1]

---

[1] "Philosophical Review," Vol. I, pp. 50-1.

PART II.

CRITICAL.

CHAPTER I.

ANALYSIS OF INTELLECTION.

§1. *The Character of the Categories.*—The character of the categories can best be shown by first stating a few erroneous views which have been set forth concerning them in philosophical literature. They are not *innate ideas*. In case there had ever been any occasion for doubt on this point, Locke's polemic would have removed it. They are not *generalizations from experience*, as Hume supposed. Kant effectually disproved this theory. They are not *generic concepts* of the highest class, under which are "subsumed" empirical concepts of lower genera, as Aristotle and Kant supposed; for that would make the categories but names for the highest generalizations of experience. Kant seemed to feel the force of this fact, and so tried to make his theory consistent by representing the categories as *forms* only, that is, as void until experience connects them with the material of sense, when they become limiting forms into which the material of sense is synthesized. Were not the inductions of experience limited by this theory of categories to a stereotyped plan of pre-conceived classification, Kant's use of the term "forms" might have been appropriate; but as he intended the categories to be used, they could be applied only to the deductions of mathematics.

The categories may now be defined as fundamental processes of thought of universal application, by means of which an object of consciousness is made to assume pairs of correlative aspects, the correlatives constituting each pair being mutually inclusive as well as mutually ex-

clusive. This can be illustrated by the category of causality. Cause and effect are contrasted aspects applied by
everyone to any and every content of consciousness. Not
that the sense-world, or any part of it, can be separated
into two parts, one being all cause and cause only,
and the other being all effect and effect only; but
every possible object of consciousness presents both aspects, cause and effect. Subordinate categories are also
characterized by the correlative principle. The terms
right and left cannot be used as mutually exclusive, without being at the same time mutually inclusive. If either
term be taken alone, it must at once be subdivided into
both right and left, or become a mere abstraction. All the
categories, both fundamental and subordinate, are processes of thought by means of which some content of consciousness is made to assume pairs of correlative aspects,
each pair of correlates being thus held in a synthesis inclusive as well as exclusive.

§2. *Deduction of the Categories.*—Three attempts have
been made to give a logical deduction of the categories,
and in each case special effort has been made to give a
complete list and to exclude all empirical elements.

KANT made the first logical deduction, which he
based entirely on Aristotle's classification of judgments.
He commended Aristotle for taking the first step in
making a list of categories, but styled his method of
enumeration as inductive, empirical and hap-hazard; but
in basing his own deduction on an inductive classification
of judgments, he rendered his method also inductive and
empirical. After completing his table of categories, Kant
proceeds to give a transcendental deduction of them, in order to show "how such concepts can *a priori* refer to objects." He does not apply his argument to any category
in particular, to show how it can so "refer to objects,"
but merely aims to show that there must be *a priori* concepts in order to make experience possible. This is really
equivalent to a surrender of all valid claim to a transcendental deduction, so far as his table of categories is concerned. In fact, *any* claim to a transcendental deduction

of categories is inconsistent, from Kant's standpoint. He made the categories "functions of unity," that is, forms for the synthesis of the manifold of phenomena. Over these *a priori* functions, as the primary function of unity, he placed the "transcendental unity of apperception." His own statements are as follows:—"If we wish to follow up the internal ground of this connection of representations to that point toward which they must all converge and where they receive for the first time that unity of knowledge which is requisite for every possible experience, we must begin with pure apperception. * * * The transcendental unity of apperception therefore refers to the pure synthesis of the imagination as a condition *a priori* of the possibility of the manifold being united in one knowledge."[1] "Only by ascribing all perceptions to one consciousness (the original apprehension) can I say of all of them that I am conscious of them. * * * It is the permanent and unchanging Ego (of pure apperception) which forms the correlate of all our representations, if we are to become conscious of them, and all consciousness belongs quite as much to such an all-embracing pure apperception as all sensuous intuition belongs, as a representation, to a pure internal intuition, namely, time."[2] This deduction of the categories identifies the "Ego (of pure apperception)" with "that point toward which they must all converge," and ascribes all perceptions to one consciousness," so as to "say of all of them that I am conscious of them." Only as a correlative of the empirical ego can this pure ego be connected in consciousness with processes of thought. Were the pure ego transcendent and separated from the empirical ego in accordance with the law of contradiction, as Kant supposed, it could give no more objective validity to "the categories, as the true fundamental concepts of the pure understanding,"[3] than it could to the *"transcendent concepts* of pure reason."[4]

---

1 "Critique of Pure Reason," Max Müller's Translation, pp. 102-3.
2 id. pp. 107-8.
3 id. p. 72.
4 id. p. 268.

FICHTE realized that Kant's deduction rested upon an induction of Aristotle's; but not having clearly perceived the nature of the principle of correlativity, he too, sought, in his deduction of the categories, to isolate the *a priori* functions of consciousness from the empirical. Fichte's starting-point is the universal pure ego, "not the knowing mind but knowledge, not an active somewhat, but an act. * * * Since among the activities to be explained consciousness also is to be found, it is self-evident that the acts to be unfolded by the Science of Knowledge do not fall within consciousness. But, for that reason, the Science of Knowledge has not to do with inventions, but its problem is to draw forth into the light the concealed mechanism by means of which consciousness is realized, that is to say, to bring into consciousness what does not fall within consciousness, because it is a *conditio sine qua non* of consciousness (hence it is called *a priori*)."[1] This position of Fichte's, like that of Kant's, renders a deduction of *a priori* categories not only impossible, but absurd, for it places the necessary starting-point beyond the reach of individual consciousness. In order "to bring into consciousness what does not fall within consciousness," Fichte starts with the principle of identity, which he has to exchange for the ego, and then again the ego for the principle of identity; consequently his thesis, antithesis and synthesis involve the processes and limitations of empirical consciousness.

HEGEL'S method of deduction was inductive rather than deductive. He started as far as possible from the concrete conscious ego, with an oscillation between the bare concepts of being and nothing; and from this oscillation deduced the category of becoming, which, when the transition is from being to nothing, passes into that of decease, and when the transition is the reverse, passes into that of origination. A continuation of this dialectic led to an inductive deduction of the whole table of categories. This dialectic of Hegel's, however, instead of isolating the *a priori* functions of consciousness from the empirical,

---

1 Erdmann, Vol. II, p. 498.

serves rather to emphasize the principle of correlativity in accordance with which the two functions are to be treated, not only as inseparable, but as mutually inclusive.

There is thus no possible transcendental or *a priori* method of deduction. The categories do not exist separate from, and cannot be separated from, empirical consciousness. The only way to discover their character, number, and relations, is to analyze empirical consciousness, and to test all processes of thought disclosed, so as to determine which are of universal validity. The only proper starting-point for the deduction of the fundamental categories is the totality of consciousness. In regard to the number of such categories, no one can say with certainty of any table, as Kant said of his, that they "completely exhaust the understanding and comprehend everyone of its faculties."[1] The following list is offered, tentatively, as setting forth in logical order only those which are fundamental. It might be called a psychological table, since it is a result of psychological analysis.

Self and Not-self.	Identity and Change.
Subject and Object.	Absolute and Relative.
Ego and Non-Ego.	Substance and Phenomena.
Unity and Plurality.	Cause and Effect.
Individuality and Universality.	Activity and Passivity.
Finitude and Infinitude.	Co-existence and Succession.

If any category can claim the first place in a logical order, it is that of self and not-self. This category must dominate every stage of finite consciousness, even though it were possible for a stage of consciousness not to be self-conscious. There can be no consciousness without some kind of self, either permanent or intermittent, either pure or composite, that perceives phenomena, and that also forms the unifying basis of all relations into which the perceived phenomena are brought. An unperceived phenomenon is a contradiction in terms; and so is a phenomenon perceived but unrelated. A series of related phenom-

---

1 "Critique of Pure Reason," p. 71.

ena with no unifying basis of relations is an absurdity; and no less absurd would it be for one of the fluent phenomena to form such a basis of fixed relations. The only basis possible for any series of fixed relations among phenomena perceived is the self that perceives and relates them. It is not the character of the self that is here in question, but the fact of the existence of the self. Whatever this self may be, whether mind or body, pure being or composite being, permanent or changeable, a perceiving self there must be; and this self must be the unifying basis with which all phenomena perceived must be correlated in in a series of fixed relations. And no less true is it that there must be, in every form of finite consciousness, a not-self which the self perceives and relates to itself. A self, perceiving only itself, would be an unrelated self, and an unrelated self must be either a nonentity or an infinity. If knowledge commenced with either a self alone or a not-self alone, the exact nature of that self or of that not-self would be known. All doubt in regard to knowledge consists in uncertainty concerning the relation of the self and the not-self; and this doubt covers every object of finite knowledge. All efforts to disclose a consciousness of a pure self as an object of knowledge, separate from a not-self, are not only futile but absurd. One of the greatest advances ever made in psychology was Kant's disclosure of the fact that neither the self nor the not-self can separately be made an object of knowledge. This is the fundamental category of consciousness; and there is no stage, form, phase, or aspect of consciousness that does not imply both the self and the not-self.   ·

After the self and the not-self have been consciously differentiated, the self assumes the character of a knowing subject, and the not-self that of an object known. These two terms are strictly correlative. Every possible content of consciousness is both subjective and objective. When any extra-organic object occupies the focus of attention, it presents both subjective and objective aspects. When such object comes in contact with a sense organ and stimulates it to activity resulting in conscious affections, the sense organ, in contrast with the stimulus, assumes the subjective aspect, and the stimulus the objective. When the contrast is between the sense organ and the conscious affections, the latter become subjective and the former objective. When the contrast is between the conscious affections and the perceiving self, the latter is subjective and the former objective. But the conscious self, when made the object of an introspective analysis, retains both aspects, that of a consciously perceiving subject and that of conscious affections objectified under the focus of attention. Only in regard to the cognitive process have the terms subjective and objective any fixed meaning. Every case of finite perception involves a subject perceiving an object, and all aspects of sense-perception involving relations antithetical to this subject and this object, are rightly termed subjective and objective. But neither the perceiving subject nor any object perceived can be viewed alone without presenting both aspects.

After the perceiving subject has distinguished itself from the object perceived, and has again differentiated the object perceived into other pairs of perceiving subjects and objects perceived, the perceiving subject assumes the character of an ego and the object perceived that of a non-ego.

In the contrast between the perceiving ego and the non-egos perceived, there arises an opposition of unity and plurality. Only in the most careless observation can the correlative nature of this opposition be overlooked. Even should the ego be identified with the body as a whole, the aspect of plurality is too marked to be overlooked; and when viewed as a mind, the ego presents such a plurality of aspects as to be mistaken by many for a collection of separate faculties. On the other hand, all the non-egos perceived are differentiations of a not-self as a unity, and can again be united by the synthetic movements of attention, into the same unity.

In so far as each conscious ego is unique, it presents the aspect of individuality, and in so far as all conscious egos are identical, they present the aspect of universality.

No ego can be entirely individual, for then it could have no fellowship with other egos, in fact, could not even be conscious of other egos. No more can an ego lack individuality, for then it would have no conscious self. The terms individuality and universality form a pair of strict correlatives.

The contrast between the limited range of individuality and the unlimited range of universality leads to the category of finitude and infinitude. Every form of finite consciousness is a manifestation of effort put forth in limitations of force, space, and time; and each of these limitations, as an object of pure thought, is characterized as infinite in both extension and divisibility, but as an object of sense, as finite in both of these respects. But an infinite extension, or quantity, is, in reality, an inconsistency; for quantity is but a limitation of the activity of a finite consciousness. For an infinite consciousness there can be no limitation, hence no limiting quantity. Neither is it the self of the finite counsciousness that is limited by quantitative relations, but the activity of the finite self in its efforts to determine the character and relations of all conscious changes. Finitude of self consists, not in being measured in terms of force, space, and time; but in being limited to change. Change in a finite consciousness implies, not the annihilation of one content of consciousness and the creation of another, but the communication of some content of consciousness from one conscious self to another. But no finite self can communicate its individuality to another finite self; it can communicate only what can be related in terms of force, space, and time. Change in a finite self thus implies, not only a universal consciousness in which changes can be related in terms of force, space, and time; but also an infinite consciousness unlimited by relations of force, space, and time; in which the individuality of every finite self realizes its own conscious existence.

The contrast between infinitude and finitude leads to that between identity and change. These terms are strict correlatives. There is nothing in the sense-world, no object of finite consciousness, that does not present both aspects, the identical and the changeable. Neither of these terms, abstracted from the other, can have any meaning. Identity means nothing but unchangeableness, and change means nothing but loss of identity.

The absolute and the relative follow as the objective support of identity and change. Identity implies an independent or absolute entity in which there is no change, hence no relation; and in correlation to this, change implies a dependent or relative entity which manifests its dependence through successive changes.

Substance and phenomena stand as the essence of the absolute and the relative. Substance is that which renders the absolute independent of all changes and relations; and as the correlate of this, phenomena are but manifestations of the relative or changeable.

The category of causality stands as the mediation between substance and phenomena. Any attempt to abstract either substance or phenomena from the other aspect discloses their necessary connection under the category of causality, in which substance appears as cause and phenomenon as effect.

Activity and passivity mediate between cause and effect in a manner similar to that in which causality mediates between substance and phenomena. Cause and effect, separated from each other, are but abstractions; and the only way in which they can be connected is to make the cause an activity of which the effect is the passive result. The correlation of activity and passivity is tersely expressed in the axiom, "action and reaction are equal and in the opposite direction."

The last category enumerated in the list, co-existence and succession, is implied in each of several of the preceding categories; yet its correlative nature is frequently overlooked. The category of causality, perhaps, illustrates this as well as any. Causation implies succession in time, yet no cause can be conceived as entirely separate from, and hence as entirely antecedent to, its effect. In arguing that these two terms are correlative, it is not meant that

a series of successive phenomena is also a series of co-existing phenomena, but that the perception of a series of terms
as forming a succession involves some form of co-existence
in consciousness of all the terms consciously related as
successive. It would be no more possible to perceive that
each of a series of terms is related in a succession, unless all
of the terms so related existed in some form in consciousness in the act of perception; than it would be to perceive
that each of a series of straight lines enters into the per-
imeter of a polygon, unless all of the lines so related were
at once present to consciousness. On the other hand,
every series of terms perceived as co-existent is perceived as
a series of terms standing in certain relations of succession under the movements of attention. Quantity of every
kind can be perceived only as successive repetitions of
some standard unit of measurement.

The nature of the subordinate categories can be indicated, and their relation to empirical concepts can be illustrated, by means of a tabular classification of the subordinate concepts.

§3. *Classification of Subordinate Concepts*—All subordinate concepts fall into two classes, inductive and
a priori, the latter being subdivided into two divisions,
the objective or real, and the subjective or ideal. Empirical
concepts have both the intellectual and the sensational
aspects, and they classify, in generic and specific relations,
all objects of sense. *A priori* concepts are characterized by
the universal aspect only; the real concepts classify objects in quantitative relations of force, space and time;
and the ideal classify all the aspects of consciousness,
fundamental and subordinate, into correlative pairs.

The fact that there is no one invariable law for deduction is much more conspicuous in the subordinate than
in the fundamental categories. The only manner of
deduction that has any resemblance to law is the rule that,
we should apply to the fundamental aspects of consciousness, the self and the not-self, such subordinate contrasts
as appear most general, and to continue the process
through successive differentiations. In this method there

is no one invariable order of differentation and no ultimate stopping-place. Kant was mistaken in supposing
that "If we are once in possession of the fundamental and
primitive concepts, it is easy to add the derivative and
secondary, and then to give a complete image of the genealogical tree of the pure understanding."[1] A "genealogical tree" may be constructed with more or less logical order,
but no one such "tree" will suit every purpose. This,
however, is no detriment to classification; for it is an ad-
vantage rather than a disadvantage for thought to be
logical and yet free from a stereotyped expression. To
show the difference between the empirical and the *a priori*
concepts, it is necessary to construct a separate "genealogical tree" for each class, as each is constructed on a different principle. One such tree will show the relation between the real and the ideal *a priori* concepts, and will
also show why the real are applicable to the classification
of the inductions of experience, while the ideal are not.
In the construction of any "genealogical tree," the logical
order most natural to the purpose in hand must be followed; and no claim to infallibility in this respect can be
made. In the two examples following, the first is designed
to illustrate the character and relation of *a priori* concepts, and the second to illustrate the mutually exclusive
relations of empirical concepts in biological classifications.
For geological, chemical or physical classifications, different principles of differentiation would be necessary. The
differentiations given in the biological tree are not intended
to follow strictly the latest biological classifications,
which are more or less conflicting, but simply to illustrate
the principle of all empirical classification and definition.

---

1 op. cit. p. 73.

INFINITE CONSCIOUSNESS.

Deductions of Consciousness.
- Finite Consciousness.
  - Self.
    - Relative or Ideal.
      - Passive State.
        - Universal Aspect, or Thought.
          - Objective Form, or Intellection.
          - Subjective Form, or Self-Consciousness.
        - Individual Aspect, or Feeling.
          - Objective Form, or Sensation.
          - Subjective Form, or ————
      - Active State, or Will.
        - Objective Form, or Volition.
        - Subjective Form, or Attention.
    - Absolute or Real.
      - Passive State, or Substance
        - Universal Aspect, or Matter.
        - Individual Aspect, or Mind.
      - Subjective Form, or Effort
        - Individual Aspect, or Action.
        - Universal Aspect, or Reaction.
  - Not-Self.
    - Absolute or Real.
      - Active State, or Force.
        - Objective Form, or Energy.
          - Individual Aspect, or Time.
            - Duration.
            - Limiting Points
              - Before.
              - After.
          - Universal Aspect, or Space.
            - Volume.
            - Limiting Surfaces.
              - Area.
              - Limiting Lines.
                - Length.
                - Limiting Points.
                  - Vertical
                    - Up.
                    - Down.
                  - Horizontal
                    - Lateral
                      - Right.
                      - Left.
                    - Longitudinal
                      - Back.
                      - Forth.
    - Relative or Ideal.
      - Active Phase, or Motive
        - Individual Aspect, or The Evil.
        - Universal Aspect, or The Good.
      - Passive Phase
        - Subjective, or Sensible Form
          - Individual Aspect, or The Ugly.
          - Universal Aspect, or The Beautiful.
        - Objective, or Intellectual Form
          - Individual Aspect, or The False.
          - Universal Aspect, or The True.

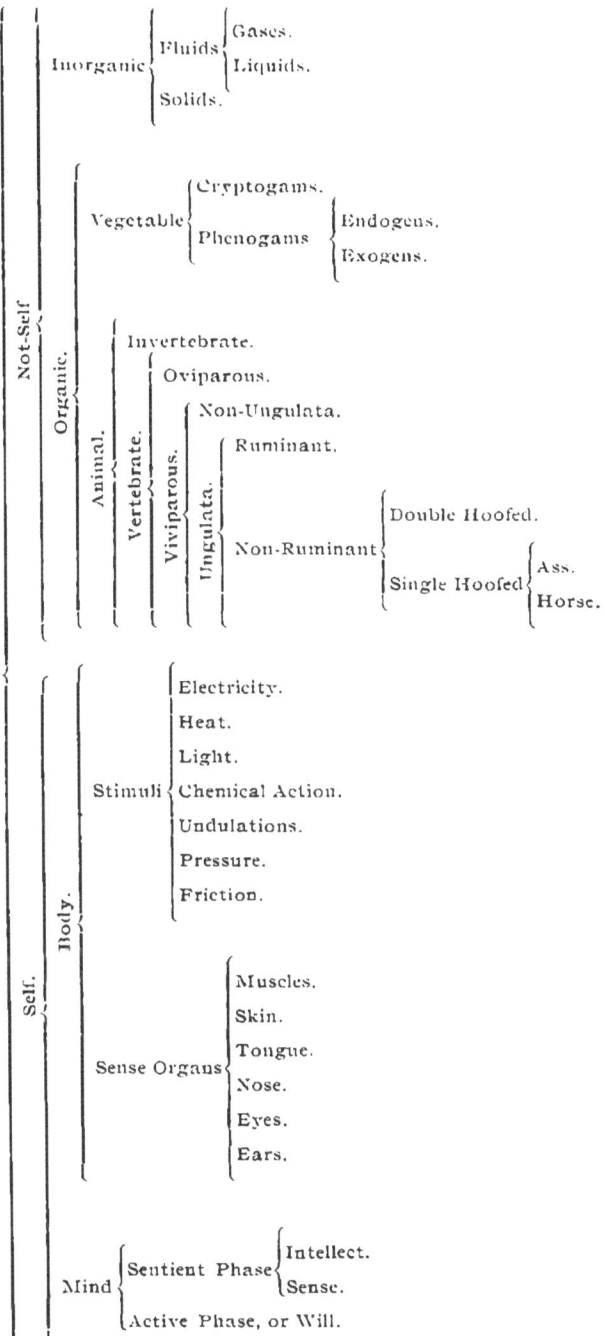

Inductions of Experience.

Not-Self

Inorganic
- Fluids
  - Gases.
  - Liquids.
- Solids.

Organic

Vegetable
- Cryptogams.
- Phenogams
  - Endogens.
  - Exogens.

Animal

Invertebrate.

Vertebrate.

Oviparous.

Viviparous.

Non-Ungulata.

Ungulata.

Ruminant.

Non-Ruminant
- Double Hoofed.
- Single Hoofed
  - Ass.
  - Horse.

Self

Body.

Stimuli
- Electricity.
- Heat.
- Light.
- Chemical Action.
- Undulations.
- Pressure.
- Friction.

Sense Organs
- Muscles.
- Skin.
- Tongue.
- Nose.
- Eyes.
- Ears.

Mind
- Sentient Phase
  - Intellect.
  - Sense.
- Active Phase, or Will.

From the classification given of *a priori* concepts, it is evident that real concepts, being based entirely upon unchanging characteristics, can be used to classify all possible objects of experience in mathematical relations, and that they can be used, in such classification, in a mutually exclusive sense; but that when they are used to classify the various aspects of consciousness as an organic unity, they must be used in a correlative sense. It is also evident that ideal concepts, notwithstanding the fact that they are universally valid, are based largely on relative, individual characteristics, and hence cannot be applied to any objects with mathematical precision.

From either classification of concepts, the *a priori* or the empirical, it will be seen that the definition of any single object of consciousness involves the construction of a "genealogical tree," which shows the successive differentiations of the totality of consciousness until all conceptions have been excluded except the one defined, and the synthesis of all the objects differentiated in their various specific and generic relations. This is shown by the position of the term *horse* in the classification of empirical concepts.

§4. *Principles of Knowledge and Laws of Thought.*—As stated on page 21, there are two fundamental principles and three primary laws governing the different processes of thought. The *principle of relativity*, as it underlies the *law of contradiction*, may be defined as that limitation of finite knowledge by virtue of which an object can be defined only by including it with all other objects differentiated in consciousness in mutual relations to one another and to consciousness as a totality and by excluding from this totality all objects not included in the definition; as it underlies the *law of mutual limitation*, it may be defined as that limitation of finite knowledge by virtue of which all incompatible aspects of any object of consciousness, when such aspects are inseparably connected with universal processes of thought, are to be attributed, · not to the object itself, but only to its appearance as determined by the limitations of finite consciousness.

The *principle of correlativity* may be defined as that limitation of finite knowledge by virtue of which an object can be defined only by referring it, as one of a pair of opposite aspects, each of which includes the existence but excludes the appearance of the other, together with all other like pairs of aspects, to the totality of consciousness as an organic unity. The *law of contradiction* applies to *empirical* and to *real a priori* concepts, the *former* including relations of both *quality and quantity*, and the *latter, only* relations of *quantity*. The *law of mutual limitation* applies only to *a priori* concepts when *different* categories came into conflict; and it is the *application* of the principle of *relativity* to such conflict. The *law of correlation*, also, applies only to *a priori* concepts; and it is the *application* of the principle of *correlativity* to them.

In the application of the law of contradiction to empirical concepts and to real *a priori* concepts, two marked differences between these two classes of concepts must be noticed. The latter, being objects of pure thought, are absolutely exclusive and infinitely divisible; while the former, being objects of sense, are only relatively exclusive and finitely divisible. Thus the *a priori* classifications of mathematics are absolutely exclusive, and the quantities of pure mathematics are infinitely divisible; while empirical classifications run together, and all sensible magnitudes cease to be perceptible after repeated division. Many long-standing inductive classifications, which were almost universally accepted, are gradually losing their distinctive character. The science of chemistry is gradually obliterating the distinction between the organic and the inorganic. The distinction between the animal and the vegetable is fading out. Between the distinct sexes, range both hermaphrodites and neuters. Inductive classifications can never be proved to be ultimate. No one knows, for example, that either oxygen or ozone is an elementary substance. No chemical element is known to be absolutely simple. Eminent scientists and philosophers who have failed to notice these differences between empirical and *a priori* concepts have violated the law of contradiction in two respects. The Eleatic philosopher Zeno based all his arguments to disprove the possibility of motion on the infinite divisibility of space as an *a priori* concept, yet he applied his arguments to sensible space. Herbert Spencer, in his discussion of the perception of space, divides magnitude into planes, planes into lines, and lines into points. This is the reverse of Zeno's error, since it carries the division of pure space to an absolute limit, while Zeno made sensible space infinitely divisible. Another error, which is a combination of these two, is committed by all scientists who argue to the indivisible atom. This error consists in carrying the division of matter past sensible limits, yet holding to the sensible qualities of matter after all sensible limits have been passed, and stopping the process of division abitrarily at an absolute limit, which, since it is past sensible limits, must be a limit to *a priori* division. Or, more strictly, this carries sensible properties past sensible limits and terminates an *a priori* process of division arbitrarily.

The law of mutual limitation is violated whenever the character of any object of consciousness is determined by one category alone, when such determination conflicts with any other fundamental category. Hegel violated this law when he maintained that "the stages which the consciousness of the individual subject passes through, have already been passed through by the universal mind."[1]

The law of correlation is violated in two ways, by representing a pair of correlates as in an antagonism which must cancel one of them, and by annulling the opposition between a pair of correlates, and so obliterating both of them. Kant's doctrine of the antinomies of pure reason is an illustration of the first error; although Kant, in the end, saves either term from being sacrificed by his doctrine of phenomena and noumena. Fichte's idealism is another illustration in which one correlate, the non-ego, was sacrificed. Schelling's "System of Identity," with its doctrine of total indifference between subject and object, is a good example of the second error.

1 Erdmann, vol. ii, p. 685.

CHAPTER II.

§1. *Sensation as sense-perception.*—This view, as stated by Locke, represents the mind, in sensation, as passive to the impress of extended objects, and the consciousness of the impression thus received, as the perception of such objects. If the mind were, in strictness, merely receptive of such impressions, it would require an actual impact of physical forces, and a corresponding impress of extended objects upon the non-extended mind. Had this fact been evident to Locke, he doubtless would have amended his theory. Three reasons may be pointed out for his failure to recognize it. First, when he represents the mind as passive, he does not conceive it as entirely passive. As has been shown, activity and passivity are strict correlates; and when either term is used, it is used in a sense not absolute but relative. Again, in tactual perception, the tactual surface receives an actual impress of extended objects, and this impress gives rise to a metaphor in which such perception is represented as an impression upon the mind. Lastly, in visual perception, the impress is refined into the convergence of rays of light upon a focal point which, losing nearly all extension, easily cheats one, who has taken the metaphor in a literal sense, into believing that an actual impression has been made upon the mind. In order to correct Locke's error, it is only necessary to realize that the human mind is necessarily both active and passive in every conscious state, that the phrase, "impression on the mind," is always necessarily metaphorical, that a non-extended mind cannot be located in any point of space, and that nothing can receive an impact of physical forces unless it be both extended and material. Locke deserves great credit for distinguishing between sensation and reflection; but not only is his distinction untenable, his method of reasoning also must be abandoned.

Berkeley improved upon Locke's account by making the mind active in sensation; but his failure to make any distinction between sense and intellect led not only to an exaggerated form of sensationalism, but also to sensational idealism, both of which have been very generally rejected.

Hume's great service consisted in establishing the fact that no knowledge of universal validity can come from sensations alone; but the answer to the scepticism thus awakened was reserved for Kant.

§2. *Sensations as subjective percepts.*—Thomas Reid, in his distinction between sensation and perception, makes a decided advance toward the true nature of the difference between them. His treatment consisted in the abstraction of the category of causality from the process of perception, and the identification of the perceptive process, as so modified, with sensation. If this distinction were made complete, by abstracting from perception all *a priori* categories, the distinction would be identical with the correlative theory. But stopping where Reid does only gives one of the various points of contrast between sense and intellect, and implies that this is all the distinction there is to be made. It is true, as Reid infers, that the category of causality characterizes perception and not sensation; but this category can be separated from the process of perception only by abstraction, and then consistency would require the abstraction of all the other *a priori* categories. To ascribe to sensation any power of perception at all, even if only of subjective affections, as Reid does, is to grant it the category of causality as well as the other categories. If his distinction be of any value, it must lie in the subjective nature ascribed to the object perceived in sensation. This point is emphasized by Hamilton.

Hamilton, while criticising Reid's form of statement, holds to the same distinction between sensation and perception. In making "the modern distinction of the Primary and Secondary Qualities of matter" correspond to the "modern distinction of the two perceptions, Perception proper and Sensation proper," he simply extends Reid's distinction to all objects of sense, and makes the distinction a little stronger by abstracting more of the *a priori* categories. But since these categories can be separated from the perceptive process only by abstraction, the process so modified would correspond to nothing found in actual experience. Yet Hamilton has in mind cases of perception in actual experience, and identifies sensation with such cases. His distinction must, therefore, if maintained, rest entirely upon the subjective character assigned to the objects perceived in sensation. His "material Non-ego" clearly implies a correlative material ego as the real basis of his "organic passion," and clearly shows that his "subject-object" is actually objectified in causal relations. As Dr. Ward says, "When considerations of method compel us to eliminate physiological implications from the ordinary conception of a sensation, we are able to distinguish the conscious subject and the affections of which it is conscious as clearly as we can distinguish subject and object in other cases of presentation."[1] The "ordinary conception," to which Dr. Ward referred, was Hamilton's. The only distinction that Hamilton can be said to have made would be, not a "distinction of the Primary and Secondary Qualities of matter," as he supposed, since his "subject-object" retains "Primary" as well as "Secondary Qualities," but a distinction between incipient and advanced stages of perception, between stages in which the objective relations of the percepts are vague and stages in which they are clear. This distinction reduces to the third form of this theory, which will be criticised in order; but that Hamilton did not have this distinction in mind is shown by the following quotation: "On the testimony of consciousness, and in the doctrine of intuitive perception, the mind, when a material existence is brought into relation with its organ of sense, obtains two concomitant, and immediate cogni-

---

1 Ency. Brit. Vol. XX, p. 41.

tions. Of these, the one is the consciousness (sensation) of certain subjective modifications in us, which we refer, as affections, to certain unknown powers, as causes, in the external reality; the secondary qualities of body : the other is the consciousness (perception) of certain objective attributes in the external reality itself, as, or as in relation to our sensible organism; the primary qualities of body. Of these cognitions, the former is admitted, on all hands, to be subjective and ideal; the latter, the Natural Realist maintains, against the Cosmothetic Idealist, to be objective and real."[1] This statement of Hamilton's, that in sense-perception the mind "obtains two concomitant and immediate cognitions," one subjective and the other objective, is an exaggerated distortion of the perceptive process in which two correlative aspects of one process are represented as two separate processes. It is impossible to divide sense-percepts into two classes, subject-objects and object-objects. An attempt to do so soon shows that every sense-percept necessarily has both aspects, the subjective and the objective, and that the two aspects are strictly correlative. The only conclusion possible is that Reid and Hamilton tried to make a distinction between sensation and perception on an untenable basis.

J. S. Mill's doctrine of sensation, when carried to its logical results, reduces both primary and secondary qualities of matter to a sensational basis, and thus reverts to Locke's sensational realism. It reduces all objects of perception to "permanent possibilities of sensation," that is, to permanent possibilities of signs of permanent possibilities, &c., ad infinitum. It also reduces sensations to signs of "permanent possibilities of sensation," that is, to signs of permanent possibilities of signs, &c., ad infinitum. It is hardly necessary to state that the view is untenable, yet, in a less explicit form of statement, it is still held very generally.

In criticising Lotze's doctrine of sensation, it is necessary first to note the different constructions that can be logically put upon his statements, for they are certainly susceptible of more than one. If his "impressions," which "exist conjointly in the soul although not spatially side by side with one another," and which the soul apprehends "not in the form in which they actually are—to-wit, non-spatial—but as they are not, in a spatial juxtaposition,"— if these impressions are the elements actually entering into and forming objects of perception; then his doctrine is a form of sensational idealism. But if, as a natural realist, Lotze makes sensations mere signs of permanent objects, each sign having an "accessory impression" for a "local sign" to determine what part of the permanent object each primary impression is to signify, then his doctrine reduces to a sensational realism still more refined than J. S. Mill's. Lotze cannot be classed with "psychic stimulists," since he believes the impressions to "exist conjointly in the soul," and to be apprehended, not directly as they are produced, but by reproduction; not as "they actually are," "but as they are not, in a spatial juxtaposition." His position seems to be anomalous. He postulates sensations after the analogy of J. S. Mill's signs, but he is not, like Mill, a natural realist. He seems to be a sensational idealist, holding objects of perception to be constructed, not upon the occurrence of sensations as stimuli to intellectual activity, but *out of* sensations. He is not of the same view as Berkeley, who made no distinction between sense and intellect; for Lotze distinguishes between the impressions and the power of the soul to act on them, and represents the impressions as passive to such action. His objects of perception are intellectual constructions, but into them the impressions enter as component factors. This form of idealism, as well as Berkeley's, is devoid of all *a priori* validity, since the constructions are determined, not by intellectual relations, but by sensations called "accessory impressions" which serve as "local signs." This doctrine would also make sensations fixed entities, like objects of perception, which is contrary to all other theories of sensation. Lotze's position, under all possible interpretations, is untenable.

J. Clark Murray confesses that a simple sensation

is undefinable, and states that "the only way a sensation can be known is by being felt." But unless it can be defined, how can one know when he feels it? To know when he feels it, he must distinguish it from other conscious states, and how can it be thus distinguished without being defined?

Sully seeks to avoid this difficulty by describing the physical conditions involved in a simple sensation; but this attempt succeeds no better. "The stimulation of the the outer extremity of an incarrying nerve," even "when this stimulation has been transmitted to the brain centers, does not always awaken consciousness. And when it does, how is the "mental state resulting from the stimulation" known to be simple? When one is conscious of the stimulation and also of the "mental state" as "resulting from the stimulation," the "mental state" is certainly not "simple" enough to be called a "mere sensation." When one is not conscious of the stimulus, how can it aid him in knowing what a simple sensation is? Moreover, the outer extremities of the incarrying nerves are not isolated, so that one can be stimulated without affecting its neighbors; but even if it were possible to stimulate separately the end-organ of one sensory nerve fibril, when it is remembered how minute such an end-organ is, it will not seem possible for such stimulation alone to be even transmitted to the brain centers. So-called sensations that can be produced and regulated by determining the character of nerve stimulation may be comparatively simple feelings; yet they can be not only defined, but measured. No such sensation is absolutely simple.

§3. *Third torm.*—Fichte argues that the first awakening act of consciousness is mere sensation devoid of all intellectual discrimination. Since this argument cannot rest on an empirical analysis of consciousness, it must be based on analogies in which the relatively complex is developed from the relatively simple. In a relative sense, mental development is an evolution of the complex from the simple; but in an absolute sense, there is not in the entire universe an ultimately simple element, either mental

or physical. Even the postulated atom has both attracting and repelling forces, quality, weight, and magnitude.
No state of consciousness can be absolutely simple, for
every such state involves a self differentiating a not-self under various *a priori* contrasts. There can be no finite consciousness that is not limited to change and identity as correlative aspects of a presentation continuum as a whole,
and of every sense-object differentiated from it. Objects of
perception become fixed, it is true, but fixed only in so far
as they are determined by *a priori* categories; in so far as
they depend upon sensation, they are constantly changing.

Dr. Ward recognizes and states the fact that in the
state of consciousness which he calls sensation, "We are
able to distinguish the conscious subject and the affections
of which it is conscious," also that "The further we go
back the nearer we approach to a total presentation having the characteristic of a general continuum in which
differences are latent." Having made sensation a presentation, he must make this primary presentation a sensation, or he would have a presentation without sensation,
a condition conceded by no one. In this first sensation,
then, are involved "a certain objective continuum" "in
which differences are latent" as well as "the conscious
subject and the affections of which it is conscious."
While these conditions do characterize the most elementary
states of consciousness, it is not proper to term such conscious states mere sensations, if a tenable distinction is to
be made between sensation and intellection. Dr. Ward's
position ascribes too much to sensation, for in the state
of consciousness specified are involved *a priori* categories.
If the distinction is claimed to be only relative, the basis
of such relative distinction must be given before it can be
intelligible. Order in time can be no basis for even a relative distinction, since the sensational and intellectual
aspects of conciousness predominate in time in very irreg-
ular order of succession. To take complexity as a basis
of distinction does not help the matter, since sensation as
well as intellection may be very complex. Activity of the
sense organs is the only basis that could be claimed for

this distinction, and the distinction could then be only relative. No consciousness can arise from mere organic action, for this would lack all *a priori* analysis and synthesis, without which consciousness cannot exist; nor, on the other hand, can any state of consciousness exist that does not involve organic action. If organic action be made the basis of a relative distinction between sensation and intellection, how is such distinction to be drawn? Who is to say where the line shall be drawn? How can uniformity of distinction as made by different individuals be secured? Of what use would such distinction be, even if it could be made uniform? Would it not be a hindrance to psychological analysis to make a distinction which would render *a priori* certainty impossible by referring all knowledge to a relatively sensational "background or basis?" Whatever relative distinction individuals may make in their own personal analyses, it is evident that no uniformity of distinction could be made on this basis of organic activity; it is also evident that no relative distinction can be of any value in psychylogical analysis.

Prof. James is explicit in making organic action the basis of his distinction between sensation and intellection; and in some of his statements he claims that the distinction is absolute. He restricts "pure sensations" to "the earliest days of life," making them "all but impossible to adults with memories and stores of associations acquired." He explicitly gives to "a new born brain an absolutely pure sensation " in which " all the 'categories of the understanding' are contained." Instead of making a distinction between sensation and intellection, this annihilates all distinction by reducing "all the categories of the understanding" to an origin in sensation. Instead of criticising this most pronounced sensational idealism, which has been regarded as utterly untenable since the time of Hume and Kant, one feels like looking further to see if the author really means what he says. In a foot-note, pp. 4-5, Vol. II, of his "Psychology," in a most excellent discussion of the relation between sensation and intellection, Prof. James shows that he meant something nearer the truth.

He says: "Psychologically, the sensory and the reproductive or associative processes may wax and wane independently of each other. Where the part directly due to
stimulation of the sense-organ preponderates the thought
has a sensational character, and differs from other
thoughts in the sensational direction. Those thoughts
which lie farthest in that direction we call *sensations*, for
practical convenience, just as we call *conceptions*, those
which lie nearer the opposite extreme. But we no more
have conceptions pure than we have pure sensations.
Our most rarefied intellectual states involve some bodily
sensibility, just as our dullest feelings have some intellectual scope. Common sense and common psychology express this by saying that the mental state is composed of
distinct fractional *parts*, one of which is sensation, the
other conception. We, however, who believe every mental
state to be an integral thing, cannot talk thus, but must
speak of the degree of sensational or intellectual character, or function of the mental state. Prof. Hering
puts, as usual, his finger better upon the truth than
any one else. Writing of visual perception, he says: 'It
is inadmissable in the present state of our knowledge to
assert that first and last the same retinal picture arouses
exactly the same *pure sensation*, but that this sensation,
in consequence of practice and experience, is differently *interpreted* the last time, and elaborated into a different perception from the first. For the only real *data* are, on the
one hand, the physical picture on the retina,—and that is
both times the same; and on the other hand, the result-
ant state of consciousness—and that is both times distinct.
*Of any third thing, namely, a pure sensation thrust in
between the retinal and the mental pictures, we know
nothing.*'" These passages from James and Hering are a
most excellent statement and illustration of the relation
between sensation and intellection. Had they made an
absolute distinction between these two correlative aspects
of every act of perception, their position would be that of
the third view; but making only a relative distinction,
based on organic action. their distinction is valueless while
their psychology is sound.

CHAPTER III.

§1. *First Form.*—This view, as it originated in Kant, rested on the only basis that made an absolute distinction between sensation and intellection possible, namely, the difference between the variable and the invariable aspects of consciousness. In making this distinction and in demonstrating its absolute validity, Kant rendered to psychology a lasting and invaluable service. He erred in not making sensation the sole function of sensibility, and in not assigning all *a priori* functions to the intellect. This, doubtless, more than anything else, prevented his distinction from being generally adopted. Sensation, however, is not a ready-made matter given to a passive mind, as Kant supposed, but a necessary aspect of every form of the activity of a finite consciousness.

Reinhold made one nominal, but not real, advance upon Kant. He united sensibility and understanding as two functions of one faculty, but he still considered the sensuous function a passive receptivity of impressions, and so made no real advance. Moreover, he failed to emphasize the distinction between sensation and intellection as resting on an *a priori* basis, and hence lost more than he gained.

§2. *Second Form.*—Mr. Spencer's use of the term "nervous shock" is not free from ambiguity, since it might refer to sudden unconscious movements in the physical organism, mere reflex actions, or to sudden conscious movements. The former, not entering consciousness, cannot be considered sensations, any more than can the sudden movements of the sensitive plant. The latter, in so far as the movements precede consciousness, are, like the former, mere reflex actions; but in so far as consciousness precedes movement, in so far as the shock is psychical, it not only follows, but also results from the perception of danger, sometimes vague, sometimes distinct. One may touch an object, either hot or cold, and shrink from it before perceiving which it is; yet, previous to this recoil, there is a perception apprehensive of danger. An apprehension of this kind may be developed by the experience of the individual or by the experience of the race, and transmitted through heredity; it results, however, in either case, from experience of danger. All nervous shocks of a psychic nature result from perception apprehensive of danger, and to identify them with sensations as units of consciousness preceding all perception, is to reverse the real order of facts. Mr. Spencer's use of the term nervous shock is so entirely based upon physical analogies that a thorough criticism of it requires the analysis of the conditions involved in nerve stimulation.

The term might refer merely to the physical stimulus, were it not identified with the "ultimate unit of consciousness." His discussion refers to normal states of consciousness in the perception of sound whose physical stimulus consists of "equal taps or blows" "not exceeding some sixteen per second." Further analysis will show that the "nervous shock" attributed to the effect of one of these blows cannot be simple, even according to Mr. Spencer's line of argument. For not only "the unlikenesses among the sensations of each class," but also "the much greater unlikenesses between the sensations of each class and those of other classes" are "due to unlikenesses among the modes of aggregation of a unit of consciousness common to them all;" "and the countless kinds of consciousness may be produced by the compounding of this element with itself and the recompounding of its compounds with one another in higher and higher degrees." According to this, the ultimate "unit of consciousness" cannot be the result of one of the "equal taps or blows" at a rate of "sixteen per second;" for in sound of the highest pitch audible, the

sound-waves strike the drum of the ear at a rate of
38,000, or more, per second, each of which must produce
a "nervous shock" and a corresponding "unit of consciousness." But even this unit, less than one two-thou-
sandth part of the one Mr. Spencer cites, must be an
aggregation. For, in referring to "tastes," "odors" and
"colors," he says, "shall we not regard it as probable that
there is a unit common to all these sharply contrasted
classes of sensations?" In the perception of violet the
undulations of ether impinge upon the retina at a rate of
over 700,000,000,000,000 per second. Can each of these
produce a "nervous shock" which will result in an ultimate "unit of consciousness?" Can 700,000,000,000,000
units of consciousness be compounded per second? If not,
if these undulations taken separately cannot be counted
as nervous shocks, if they must be summed together in
order to give rise to a "unit of consciousness," how can
the number which must be summed together be determined? If this number be determined by the number of
conscious changes that can be discriminated per second,
the number must be different not only for different persons
but for different sense-organs in the same person. Either
over 700,000,000,000,000 "units of consciousness" must
be compounded per second, or stimuli must be summed
together in the production of conscious states. If the
number of "ultimate units of consciousness" cannot exceed "some sixteen per second," the number of stimulat-
ing disturbances represented by each must exceed 40,000,-
000,000,000. But inasmuch as the number of percepts
discriminated per second varies with the person, with the
sense-organ, and with the practice of the individual; it
must be concluded that the number of nerve disturbances
involved in the stimulation of the nerves has no intelligible bearing upon the number of states of consciousness
resulting from such stimulation. Spencer's position is
similar to that of Hamilton, who in the following pas-
sage argues that conscious states are composed of unconscious states: "When we look at a distant forest, we perceive
a certain expanse of green. Of this, as an affection of our

organism, we are clearly and distinctly conscious. Now, the expanse of which we are conscious, is evidently made up of parts of which we are not conscious. No leaf, perhaps no tree, may be separately visible. But the greenness of the forest is made up of the greenness of the leaves,; that is, the total impression of which we are conscious, is made up of an infinitude of small impressions of which we are not conscious."[1]

Whatever force this argument may seem to have must be claimed from the stand-point of natural realism, the position maintained by both Hamilton and Spencer. But from this very point of view the argument can be disproved on both empirical and *a priori* grounds. Scientific experiments show that the impression made by the sight of a word is not composed of the several impressions made by the sight of the letters separately, for words can be distinguished in consciousness nearly as rapidly as can letters. Again, if a certain force will move a body at a certain velocity, then, according to Hamilton's argument, a part of the force would impart a corresponding rate of velocity. But a part of the force may not overcome the inertia, and so may not impart any velocity to it. In like manner, a certain stimulation may awaken consciousness when a part of the stimulation will not. This can be verified by anyone at pleasure. It is much more rational to suppose that a stimulus below a certain limit fails to awaken consciousness at all than to suppose that it awakens an unconscious state of consciousness. To suppose a conscious state to be composed of unconscious states is just as absurd as to suppose an extended object to be composed of non-extended parts. When quantitative zeros can be summed together and made to produce extended quantities, then it may do to argue that unconscious zeros may be summed together and made to produce conscious states; but not before.

The "deceptions," or "mistakes," mentioned in Fick's experiments, are based not upon an uncertain compounding of "units of feeling," but upon the reference of a com-

---

[1] Mill's "Philosophy of Sir William Hamilton," Vol. II., p. 10.

plex state of feeling to that cause which would seem most likely to awaken the feeling. Sensations of touch and temperature are so intimately connected that, in normal experience, neither one is felt without the other. Sensations of temperature can be located only by means of related tactual sensations. That there should be four deceptions out of seven stimulations "on the lumbar spine," a region of little discriminative power for either sensation, ís not surprising, especially when the attention is adjusted for the perception of both. Four mistakes "in a series of 60 stimulations" on the back of the hand is better than could be expected. But when it is remembered that "there was never any deception on the entire palmar side of the hand or on the face," it seems to be evidently a matter of developed discrimination and association, and not of a mixture of "units of feeling."

Mr. G. H. Lewes carries the analysis of the physical conditions of sensation far past anything reached yet; but even he can not claim to have reached ultimate elements, since he stopped with "the movements of the psychoplasm" which "constitute sensibility." These "tremors" of the Psychoplasm," which he terms "neural units, the raw material of consciousness," must be exceedingly numerous and minute; yet they cannot be either ultimate or raw. Whatever the "Psychoplasm" may be, these "tremors" must contain all the disturbances of all the end-organs of all the nerves of all the sense-organs in all the various forms of stimulation. In each retina there are estimated to be 1,000,000 end-organs. Undulations of light impinge upon these at rates varying from 400,000.000,000,000 to 700,000,000,000,000 per second. A fair average would be at least 500,000,000,000,000 per second. Multiplying the number of end-organs in both retinæ by this average would give 1,000,000,000,000,000,000,000,000 retinal disturbances per second. But each of these "tremors" involves very many "molecular movements;" and so, to reach the ultimate component disturbances of the "Psychoplasm," another large multiplication must be made. Yet even this inconceivably great product will give neither ultimate "neural units" nor "raw material." These molecular "neural units" are not only compound, being resultants of atomic movements, but inasmuch as heat is always evolved in chemical synthesis, this "material of consciousness" must have been cooked in the process. To reach the ultimate "raw material of consciousness," it is necessary to compute the attracting and repelling forces of the atoms. This, however, is the ultimate "raw material," not of sense, but of nonsense.

CHAPTER IV.

§1. *Review.*—Green's position is most positive and explicit in denying the existence of "such a thing in the world of phenomena" as "mere sensations antecedent to any action of the intellect; but he uses the term sensation whenever it suits his convenience to do so. Yet he not only fails to give a clear distinction between sensation and "action of the intellect;" but the following statements indicate that such distinction was not clear in his own mind. "We conclude, then, that facts of feelings, as perceived, are not feelings as felt; that, though perception presupposes feeling, yet the feeling only survives in perception as transformed by a consciousness, other than feeling, into a fact which remains for that consciousness when the feeling has passed."[1] "Only because we do more than feel—only because we think in feeling, and thus feel *objects*—have we any need of words. Hence we have talked of seeing and touching things long before we have reflected on the visual and tactual feelings which are the conditions of our seeing and touching them. When we come thus to reflect, we have no words for the feelings, but the same which we have applied to the perceptions conditioned by but essentially different from them; and under the illusion caused by this usage, we are brought to think that the visual and tactual sensations are equivalent to the perceptions which we call by the same names. It, requires, therefore, a certain effort to convince ourselves that it is possible to have a visual sensation without seeing anything, and a tactual sensation without being conscious of touching anything; and, conversely, that

---

1. "Works," Vol. I, p. 412.

what I am said to see never is or includes a visual sensation, nor what I am said to touch a tactual sensation."[1]

These passages imply that "a consciousness other than feeling" might exist apart from feeling; "that 'facts of feeling' as perceived" might be devoid of "feelings as felt;" that "feelings as felt" might be unperceived; and that feeling might be "transformed by a consciousness other than feeling into a fact that remains—when the feeling is passed." Green states "that it is possible to have a visual sensation without perceiving anything — and conversely, that what I am said to see never is or includes a sensation." Again he states "to feel warm then is not the same as to perceive that I am warm,"[2] and "Hence our habit of overlooking the essential difference between the 'phenomenon' as it issues from the process of attention—the proper object of perception—and the sensation which precedes that process, or of any of the sensations which accompany it."[3]

In some of these statements Green seems to assume Hamilton's position, making sensation a perception of secondary qualities. In making sensations precede the "process of attention," he seems to take J. S. Mill's position. But his own positive statements repudiate both of these views. Hence by "feelings as felt" he must have meant sensations; and by "consciousness other than feeling," "action of the intellect." Feeling cannot be "transformed" into anything "other than feeling," and the "fact that remains for that consciousness" is the fact that the self remembers and continues to feel. Feeling is fluent, facts are fixed. There can be no fluent feeling that is not perceived as a fixed fact, neither can there be fixed facts, the perception of which does not involve fluent feeling. Fluent feeling could not be transformed in the act of perception and still be perceived as fluent. Again it is impossible "to have a visual sensation without seeing anything," unless the "seeing" be restricted to discriminate

---

1 op. cit., p. 414,
2 id, p. 414.
3 id, p. 415.

perception; and when it is so limited it should be so
stated. The statement, "what I am said to see never is or
includes a visual sensation," is true, but misleading. No object perceived is composed of mere sensations; it is a product
resulting from a conscious activity of which sensation is but
an inseparable function. To say that an object of perception "never is or includes sensation" is equivalent to saying that a fixed identity objectified under a priori categories in unchanging relations never is or includes change.
Green's statement is, in reality, a sort of figure of speech;
a figure confusing, yet frequent in that part of psychological literature which treats of sensation. The figure really
involves two pairs of correlatives, yet the contrast is made
between two terms, one of which belongs to each pair.
Change and identity are correlative aspects of every *object*
of perception, and sensation and intellection are corresponding correlative aspects of every *act* of perception.
In speaking of sense-objects it is customary to refer to the
aspect of identity alone and to regard the aspect of change
as characterizing only the perceptive process In this way
the object, spoken of as "what I am said to see," is represented as a fixed identity independent of its correlative
change; and in contrast with this object, misrepresented
in this figure of speech as unchanging, is placed the term
sensation, misrepresented also as being independent of its
correlative intellection. It is unfortunate to use technical terms in a figurative sense, or in a loose popular
way, or without accepting or giving any definition of
them; also to make statements general when they are
true only in a restricted sense. And it is inconsistent, to
say the least, to err in both respects, after having been
severely critical of the same errors in others.

But Prof. Green has carried the analysis of conscious
phenomena farther than it had ever been carried before;
and consequently, either new terms must be used, or old
terms must be used in a more restricted sense. He has established the fact that all classifications of the phenomena
of consciousness must be based, not upon the principle of
relativity, but upon that of correlativity. This requires a

constant discrimination on the part of a writer, between the relative and the correlative signification of such terms as feeling and sensation, and a corresponding qualification of statement, both of which are all but impossible to those who first make the distinction. The criticism to which Prof. Green has left himself open is that his statements fail to do justice to his thought.

Dr. Dewey distinguishes very clearly between feeling and thought, making the former the individual aspect and the latter the universal aspect of consciousness. He does not, however, define sensation so as to show its relation to feeling. This will be done later.

Prof. Ladd emphasizes the facts that "there are no sensations (whatever physical occasion of sensation may exist) except those that exist in consciousness;" that "the simple sensation is a necessary fiction of psycho-physical science;" and that psychology "analyzes what is relatively complex into what is relatively very simple and elementary." This precludes the view which holds to unconscious infinitessimal sensations, also the view that sensations may be given independently of all intellectual activity; and it at the same time justifies the use of the term sensation in psychological analysis.

§2. *Definition and Illustration.*—In every form of consciousness there are involved, as before stated, both *a priori* categories, and fluent states of feeling. When the perceptive process is dominated principally by the *a priori* categories, the percepts assume the form of quantitative relations of force, space, and time; but when dominated principally by the flow of feeling, so-called subjective percepts of sound, color, taste, smell and feeling occupy the attention. In both cases of perception there are involved both, categories, or the universal element, and feeling, or the individual element. The percepts of force, space, and time have meaning only as causing, containing, and ordering the subjective percepts; and the subjective percepts can be defined only as they are related causally, spatially, and temporally. In illustrating this difference between sensation and intellection, it is customary to refer to the ex-

periences of earliest infancy, as being chiefly sensational.
But since this early experience cannot be recalled in memory, it becomes necessary to adopt some method of producing an experience which is supposed to be characterized principally by sensation.   Thus, by inhaling anæs-
thetics, one can gradually reduce the whole field of consciousness through a series of indistinct, confused, and
fading presentations, to a fluent blur, in which forms, colors, sounds, and all other percepts are dissolved in a
flickering, vanishing continuum, which, so long as consciousness lasts, continues to be a changing, fading object
of attention.   Anyone disliking to follow this method can
try another which, though not so effectual, will illustrate
pretty well the same facts.   By focusing the attention
steadily upon a fixed point in the field of vision, the whole
field may be gradually reduced to a glimmering sheen, in
which forms and colors blend together, only to start forth
again on the least movement of the attention from one
to another of the main points which are constantly vanishing or emerging from the visual field.   So soon as the
focus of attention is moved from one point to another,
the whole field assumes a new and distinct phase, which,
if the attention be again held fixed, fades as before.   In
normal perception, the attention is allowed free movement; and the presentation, rapidly changing from one
fixed phase to another, is synthesized into an object,
which, although constantly changing, is regarded as
changed in appearance only, that is, the change is regarded as subjective, and a fixed identity is ascribed to the
object.   The movements of attention emphasize the fixed
phases of the presentation which are regarded as different
appearances of an unchanged object.   In this analysis of
perception there must be noted (1) the constantly changing, vanishing, and emerging aspects of the field of consciousness, giving way, under (2) the movements of attention, to (3) fixed phases of the presentation continuum.   The perceptive process is thus always both analytic
and synthetic, that is, it differentiates the presentation
continuum into analytic data under the movements of at-

tention, and automatically and instantaneously synthesizes these analytic data into complex "presentations of sense." The three facts, changing aspects,
movements of attention, and fixed phases, are involved in every state of finite consciousness; and,
though it may at first seem impossible, they are
simultaneous. It at first seems that the changing
aspects precede the movements of attention and cause
them, also that the movement of attention consists in a
series of starts and stops, and that each stop is followed
by a fixed phase of the presentation. More careful observation, however, will show that the attention is in constant movement, moving more or less rapidly at times,
and hence appearing at times more or less fixed, but never
absolutely fixed. Moreover, the movements of attention
may be considered the cause of the changing aspects just
as logically as the effect of them. The eye moves voluntarily and involuntarily, and voluntary movement frequently seems to be composed of starts and stops; yet
the eye cannot be held absolutely fixed, as anyone can
verify by trial. The attention moves in harmony not with
the action of the eye alone, but with the action of every
sense-organ, both voluntarily and involuntarily. Like the
movements of the eye, the voluntary movements of attention seem composed of starts and stops. When, however,
any apparently single and separate movement of attention is carefully examined, it proves to be, like every other
presentation, a continuum of still lower analytic data;
and this fact holds true indefinitely. This shows not that
a conscious state can be held under the focus of attention
and subjected to an infinite process of division into
infinitessimal elements approximating to zeros of consciousness; but that no fixed states of consciousness
exist, and that the so-called analysis is a process of constant change in which the component elements are but
moments. The vanishing and emerging aspects of the presentation may precede certain voluntary movements of attention, but they cannot precede all movements of attention and be in consciousness at all. The changing aspects,

the movements of attention, and the fixed phases of the presentation are simultaneous and correlative factors of every state of finite consciousness, in which consciousness there are no absolutely fixed, unchanging elements separ· ated in time. In the process of perception, consciousness constructs fixed objects of sense upon the differentiations of the continuum, regarding each object as a synthesis of fixed component elements, each of which in turn is again regarded as composed of still lower analytic data, and so on *ad infinitum*. Every possible sense-object thus becomes, under the movements of attention, according as the move- ment is synthetic or analytic, either an analytic compon- ent element of a higher continuum, or a synthetic contin- uum of lower analytic data. There is no ultimate stopping- place in consciousness where the analytic data can be, or correspond to, simple sensations or ultimate units of con- sciousness. The three characteristics of consciousness, changing aspects, movements of attention, and fixed phases of the presentation, correspond to the (1) individ- ual element related through (2) functions of the will to (3) the universal element. Thus, corresponding to the indi- vidual and the universal elements, are the two aspects of the sentient phase of consciousness termed, respectively, feeling and thought; and these two phases are related to each other through the motive phase, the will. Each of these factors of consciousness, feeling, thought, and will, according as it is referred to the ego or the non-ego, as- sumes a subjective or an objective form. The subjective form of the will, the adjustment of the ego to the non-ego, is attention; the objective form, the adjustment of the non-ego to the ego, is volition. The subject- ive form of thought is self-consciousness, the ob- jective form is intellection. The subjective form of feeling is, as yet, without a name, except as it is referred to as pleasure and pain. A very appropriate and convenient name for it would be *pathy*, by which name it will be designated hereafter in these pages. The objective form of feeling is sensation. Prof. Bain expresses this fact very neatly as follows: "A sensation is, properly speaking, a sensum, a phase of our objective consciousness."[1] This, of course, as has been repeatedly stated, does not mean that so-called subjective percepts, such as colors, sounds and tastes, are sensations; for all such percepts involve the *a priori* principles of intellection as well as sensation. In so far as such percepts can be described in terms of universal application, giving causal, spatial and temporal relations, they involve the *a priori* principles of intellection; and in so far as their character is variable for each individual perceiving subject, in so far as they can be described only by comparing them with one another, when such comparison is not known to be identical for all perceiving subjects, they involve sensation. Sensation and intellection cannot be regarded as component elements of sense-objects. In so for as sense-objects can be analyzed, they are composed of lesser sense-objects; and their different qualities, such as form, color, taste, etc., are but their appearances to different sense-organs, singly or in groups, each of which appearances involves both sensation and intellection. Consciousness is a unity; and the sense-world is a continuum, complex in its differentiations. Yet each object gets meaning only as it is related to the whole continuum. Consciousness cannot begin in disconnected states of any kind. To be conscious is to be a unity, conscious of a continuum; and the presentation continuum, in its earliest stages, is a complex unity presenting both aspects, sensation and intellection.

In giving final definitions to psychological terms, it is necessary to notice the double use made of many of them. The same term is used to denote either an activity of consciousness, or the product resulting from such activity. In some cases kindred terms are used, such as conception and concept, perception and percept. The nature of sense, sensation, intellect and intellection, and also their relation to each other and to consciousness as a whole, can best be shown by the following tabulation:

---

1   "The Senses and Intellect," 3d Ed., p. 382.

					INFINITE.					
					Motive Phase, or Will.					
CONSCIOUSNESS	FINITE	Sentient Phase, or Intelligence.	Individual Aspect, or Feeling.	Active State, or Sense. Passive State or Sensibility.	Attention.	Form, or Subjective	Volition.	Form, or Objective	Pathy.	Sensation.	Process.	Product.
			Universal Aspect, or Thought.	Active State, or Intellect. Passive St., or Intellectuality					Self-Consciousness.	Intellection.	
				Cause.					Effect.		

In the above tabulation, every term represents consciousness as a unity, viewed in some correlative phase, aspect, form, or state; e. g., "Sensation" represents consciousness in the objective form of the individual aspect of the sentient phase.

In addition to the generic meaning of the term sensation, as indicated in this tabulation, it has two specific meanings which are of frequent use. In psycho-physical measurements, it is used to designate a simple percept of any single sense; and in psychological analysis it is used to designate any least possible change in the sensational aspect of the presentation continuum. It would be well if the term percept could supplant the use of the term sensation in all psycho-physical measurements, for then the term sensation would have but one generic and one specific meaning, and all ambiguity would thus be avoided.

PART III.

CHAPTER I.

§ 1. *Limits to Physical Analysis.*—In passing from
the mental to the physical conditions of sensation, one
might at first expect to pass from the changeable to the
fixed. Such expectation, however, if entertained, soon
vanishes. In a certain sense the physical is more fixed
than the mental; but in the physical conditions of sensation there is such an endless complexity of detail, forever
dissolving before a critical analysis into still lower minutiæ,
that no fixed limit can be named from which to start
definition and classification. The only ultimate starting-
place would be the atom of matter and the undulation of
force; but these are entirely beyond empirical analysis, and
so are even less satisfactory than the ever changing presentations of consciousness.

§ 2. *Doubtful Problems.*—Doubt exists concerning the
number of senses and the character of the functions of
some of them. The so-called sense of touch includes
several senses, the number and character of which are
still undetermined. The existence of three, the tactual,
the muscular, and the thermal, appears to be established
beyond reasonable doubt. Two others, the sense óf the
articular cartilages and the sense of innervation, are still
in dispute.

Doubtful points concerning the exact nature of nerve-
stimuli can probably never be determined. The nature of

the photo-chemical process, by which the rods and cones of the retina are supposed to be stimulated, is beyond the reach of even intelligent guessing. In what manner we perceive the direction from which sounds come, is a question involving complex difficulties. The differences between normal and abnormal stimulation cannot always be determined. Every problem of physiological psychology involves undetermined factors and indeterminable conditions.

§3. *Changes of Nervous Tissue.*—Chemical change is constantly taking place in all the tissues of the body; but there is reason to believe that in nerve-stimulation such change is unusually rapid in both brain and nerves. "On general principles of physical science there can be little doubt that the excitation and conduction of nerve-commotion is dependent upon a chemical change in the nervous tissue itself. Moreover, we know that the process of conduction in the nerve requires each of its molecules to act upon the neighboring elements as the condition of the process continuing. Nor can this process itself be a mere impartation of motion, from molecule to molecule; on the contrary, the phenomena of electrotonus seem to show that it must also consist in the setting free of energy which exists latent within the molecules of the nerve-substance. Accordingly, we should be tempted to describe the process of progressive excitation of the nerve somewhat as follows: Every element of the nerve, by reason of its highly complex and unstable chemical constitution, contains a large store of energy; the excitement of the nerve consists in the explosive decomposition successively of these elements of the nerve; and the result of the decomposition is the setting free of the stored energy to be expended in part in the excitation of the next adjoining elements. The process, then, is not altogether unlike the burning of a line of powder grains. Such an hypothesis, however, would at once have to answer several difficult questions. Why does not the whole of the explosive substance burn up instead of only an amount of it approximately proportional to the strength of the stimulus which sets the process agoing?"[1]

§4. *The Psyco-physical Law.*—The relation between strength of stimulus and intensity of sensation is determined by actual experiment and stated in the so-called "psycho-physical law." The strength of the stimulus can easily be determined in regard to the senses of sight, hearing, and touch; but since the intensity of the sensation always involves a subjective estimate, no invariable law is possible. The general law holds, that the ratio of increase in the stimulus is greater than the ratio of increase in the intensity of the sensation. In general, the more intense the sensation, the less sensitive is the judgment to slight changes in intensity; hence (since intensity cannot be measured objectively, but can only be estimated subjectively), it naturally follows that the ratio of successive changes in intensity is less than that of the corresponding changes in the strength of stimulus.

Prof. James uses the term, "elementary psycho-physic law," to express "the connection of thought and brain" when "stated in an elementary form." He says: "As the total neurosis changes, so does the total psychosis change." "Every sensation corresponds to some cerebral action. For an identical sensation to recur it would have to occur the second time *in an unmodified brain.*" "Before the connection of thought and brain can be explained, it must at least be *stated* in an elementary form; and there are great difficulties about so stating it. To state it in an elementary form one must reduce it to its lowest terms and know which mental fact and which cerebral fact are, so to speak, in immediate juxtaposition. We must find the minimal mental fact whose being reposes directly on a brain-fact; and we must similarly find the minimal brain-event which will have a mental counterpart at all. Between the mental and physical minima thus found there will be an immediate relation, the expression of which, if we had it, would be the elementary psycho-physic law."[2]

---

1. Ladd's "Phys. Psy." pp. 222-3.
2. "Principles of Psychology," vol. I, pp. 243, 232, and 177.

The "minimal mental fact," in the form of an "ultimate unit of consciousness," proved to be a mere fiction; and the minimal "neural unit," in the "raw material of consciousness," proved likewise to be a mere product of the imagination. But if it be true that "For an identical sensation to recur it would have to occur the second time in an unmodified brain" (and no one seems ever to have disputed or doubted the statement), it would require, in order to fully state "the connection of thought and brain," a complete physical and chemical analysis of both brain and nerves, setting forth all conditions and changes for each successive sensation. This would be the "minimal brain-event" involved in "the elementary psycho-physic law" of which Prof. James speaks.

Any psycho-physical law that pretends to express in mathematical terms a causal relation between the physical and the psychical involves undetermined factors, indeterminable conditions, and unverifiable assumptions.

CHAPTER II.

§1. The muscular sense is so inseparably associated with the tactual, that its exact nature can probably never be determined. That it has a distinct character cannot reasonably be doubted, since the presence of both sensory nerve-fibrils and motor end-plates in the muscles warrants the conclusion that the sense of effort is dependent upon the muscular sense for its intensive character. The sense of effort seems to be attributed by different psychologists to at least four different sources, stimulation of tactual nerves, of afferent nerves in the muscles, of the motor end-plates of the efferent nerves to the muscles, and to central innervation. Bain, Wundt, Helmholtz and others claim the existence of a sense of central innervation; Ferrier, Ladd, James and others dispute the existence of such a sense, and claim that the sense of effort is due chiefly to kinaesthetic tactual sensation. James argues the question very forcibly from three different stand-points, the "*a priori*," the "introspective," and the "circumstantial." The *a priori* argument is that such a sense could be of no value, inasmuch as the movements causing all desired changes in sensation are associated with the kinaesthetic sensations accompanying such changes, and these sensations furnish the only cue needed for the proper control of the necessary movements. Arguing from the "introspective" point of view, James says:—"*There is no introspective evidence of the feeling of innervation. Whenever we look for it and think we have grasped it, we find that we have really got a peripheral feeling or image instead—an image of the way in* which we feel when the innervation is over, and the movement is in process of doing or is done. * * * There is indeed the fiat, the element of consent, or resolve that the act shall ensue. This, doubtless, to the reader's mind, as to my own, constitutes the essence of the voluntariness of the act. * * * No one will pretend that its quality varies according as the right arm, for example, or the left is used. *"An anticipatory image, then, of the sensorial consequences of a movement (plus on certain occasions), the fiat that these consequences shall become actual, is the only psychic state which introspection lets us discern as the forerunner of our voluntary acts."*[1] This same thought has been expressed by Dr. Dewey as follows: "Our experience consists in learning to interpret these sensations; in seeing what acts they stand for. Having learned this, knowing that a certain sensation means a certain movement, we control the movement by controlling the sensations. We learn, in other words, not only the meaning of a sensation, but the connection of the various sensations, and in what order sensations must be arranged in order to occasion other sensations."[2] Anyone can easily convince himself of the truth of the above statements by noting facts in his own experience. For example, while one is reading, some spot on the surface of the body may suddenly give rise to sharp, stinging sensations; when, without thought of a muscle or a movement, the hand will find the spot and relieve the pain. What is willed in such cases is not an innervation, not a movement, but a change of sensations; and this causes the movements necessary to make the desired changes.

From the "circumstantial" point of view it is argued that in all examples cited as cases of innervation, the feeling in question proves to be a complex of peripheral sensations; and that there are conclusive reasons for believing such to be necessarily always the case. Wundt argues that, were the feeling of effort of peripheral origin, it ought always to be proportional to the work actually

---

1. "Principles of Psychology," Vol. II., pp. 499-501.
2. Psychology, p. 375.

done, and that this is not the case. A person may feel great effort in trying to move a limb partially paralyzed when but little or no movement follows. These facts, he claims, show a central origin of the feeling. Against these arguments, it is claimed that in all such cases where a sense of effort is felt, there is actual muscular contraction of the respiratory muscles, especially of the glottis, and that the feeling of effort always accompanies such contraction; but that if this be prevented, and no other muscular contraction occurs, no sense of effort can be felt. It is very natural to contract the respiratory muscles in all cases of absorbed attention. In listening intently one is apt to stop breathing, and this occasions a sense of effort; but if natural breathing be maintained while listening, no such sense of effort will be noticed. The only histological evidence of the existence of a sense of innervation is the motor end-plates in the efferent nerves; but this would argue for a peripheral not a central sense. A peripheral sense of this nature might arise, but it would always be inseparably associated with the efferent muscular sense. And as Prof. Ladd says, "we seem warranted in assuming that there is no such specific difference in the function of the two kinds of nerves as is dependent upon the peculiar structure or molecular processes of each kind. Both afferent and efferent nerves are probably capable of the same kind of molecular commotion called nervous excitation, and of conducting this commotion in either direction. The marked difference in the results of the exercise of this function in the two cases is probably due chiefly to the difference in the organs from which the excitation of the nerve starts, and into which it is discharged."[1] From all the facts stated it would seem most rational to suppose that the sense of effort is, in so far as its intensity is concerned, dependent upon the muscular sense, which is peripheral in origin and connected with the stimulation of both afferent and efferent nerves. In so far as spatial relations are associated with the sense of effort, this sense is doubtless dependent upon the tactual sense.

---

1. "Phys. Psy." pp. 54-5.

§2. The sense of touch seems to be the next sense in the order of development. Aside from its relation to the muscular sense, there seems to be little doubt regarding its character. It is sharply distinguished from the sense of temperature; and the only remaining source of doubt seems to be its relation to the sense of the articular cartilages. Although histology has done nothing as yet to determine the presence of nerve end-organs in these cartilages, the sense of feeling connected with them is probably a form of the tactual sense connected with the synovial membrane reflected upon the marginal surfaces of the joints.

§3. The sense of temperature has been represented as a double sense, having both "heat-spots" and "cold-spots." The separate existence of such spots possibly depends upon the fact that some regions of the skin come more frequently into contact with objects warmer than themselves, while with other regions, the reverse is true. "Sensations of temperature have apparently, a certain dependence on the temperature of the thermic apparatus itself. This law has been elaborated and defended in detail by Hering in the following form: 'As often as the thermic apparatus at any spot in the skin has a temperature which lies above its own zero-point we have a sensation of heat; in the contrary case, a sensation of cold.' By the 'zero-point' of any part of the skin is meant the exact objective temperature which at that part will produce no sensation of either heat or cold. Such zero-point is, of course, different for different parts of the body, according as they are or are not exposed, and are or are not well supplied with arterial blood."[1]

§4. The sense next in order of differentiation is taste. It is definitely located and has special nerve-branches and specific nerve-endings. Since the tongue is the chief organ of taste, and also well adapted by its form and situation to act as an organ of both touch and temperature, it naturally follows that sensations of touch and temperature are often confused with sensations of taste. So-called pungent tastes are tactual affections; and cooling tastes, like

---

1. Ladd's "Phys. Psy." p. 350.

that of peppermint, are greatly modified by the sense of temperature. From the close proximity and kindred nature of the sense of taste to that of smell, odors are frequently confused with tastes. So-called flavors are principally olfactory affections.

§5. In the sense of smell a degree of differentiation is reached which is characterized by a separate cranial nerve and a separate sense-organ. The only confusion in regard to the function of the sense of smell is the possible confusion with the sense of taste.

§6. The sense of sight has its own special cranial nerve and its own separate sense-organ; but as this organ has also a very finely discriminating sense of movement, retinal sensations are greatly modified by the concomitant tactual and muscular sensations.

§7. The auditory sense-organ is the most completely differentiated and isolated of all, being enclosed in a bony cavity and removed from all the disturbing influences to which the other senses are liable. And yet even this sense, shut in as it is, is modified in its function by changes in its stimulus resulting from the varying conditions of the surrounding tissues and fluids. Respiration, pulsations of the heart, and the varying pressure of blood-vessels and air passages, both normal and abnormal, affect the undulations that stimulate the auditory end-organs.

§8. The senses thus entitled to scientific recognition as primary, special senses, are the muscular sense, and the senses of touch, temperature, taste, smell, seeing and hearing. The specific quality of the sensations of four of these senses, and the variations of such quality, are noted and named. Sounds are high and low; colors are violet, indigo, blue, green, yellow, orange and red; tastes are sweet, sour, salt and bitter; temperatures are warm and cold. In this respect the other three senses are less fortunate. Odors and tactual and muscular sensations are so closely associated with corresponding physical objects that they can be named only in connection with those objects. This does not lessen their practical value, however, since consciousness recognizes them and passes to their significates as readily as though each had a separate name.

§1. *Mental.*—Attention is an important factor in determining the character of sensation. A listener to music may follow the soprano, tenor, alto, or bass separately; or he may follow the combined result, regardless of the different parts. But what he hears in the latter case is not a mixture of what he might have heard, following the parts separately. One having no knowledge of music cannot follow the parts separately; while one skilled in music can hardly help doing so more or less, can, in fact, hardly hear music as he did before he had learned to analyze it. Again, a person listening intently cannot see so well, or looking intently, cannot hear so well; his sensations are, in either case, different from what they would be were his attention not pre-occupied. At every movement of the attention, the whole presentation changes, new elements being constantly differentiated and as rapidly synthesized. This is not a mere division of the same presentation into new parts, but every such differentiation renders the whole presentation new.

Expectation greatly modifies the differentiation and the synthesis. When changes are expected, they frequently appear without objective causes, or with none sufficient to give rise to them as seen. In twilight, people frequently see, not real objects before them, but creations of their own imagination.

A priori principles, such as substantiality, causality, identity and the various spatial and temporal categories, dominate all minds alike in ascribing to the presentation an independent reality fixed in permanent relations of force, space, and time. "Things are known only through the sensations which they produce in us; and how can we pass from these sensations to the notion of things extended in space? Moreover, sensations are in perpetual flow; how can we pass from their constant change to the changeless relations of space?"[1] In order to maintain the conception of things as unchanged in space, in opposition to all the testimony of the senses that the objective world in every part is in constant change, intellection, especially with the a priori categories of identity and substantiality, accounts for all changes as effecting appearance only and not substance. When things disappear entirely from view and reappear again, consciousness unavoidably concludes that there is something supersensible, either magnitudes or substances or forces. These metaphysical postulates are then regarded as unchanging, and as constituting the basis of all fixed objects related in time and space.

§2. *Physical.*—"As the total neurosis changes, so does the total psychosis change." The physical conditions involved in the "neurosis" may be analyzed into component elements more or less fixed, and this naturally gives rise to the impression that the conscious data involved in the "psychosis" may also be analyzed in a similar manner into fixed component elements. While there is a certain correspondence between the analyses of the neurosis and of the psychosis, there is an essential difference between the two. A certain sensation may follow the stimulation of a sense-organ. Both the stimulation and the sense-organ may be analyzed into separate component elements. and a different sensation may result from a partial stimulation of the sense-organ. The latter sensation, however, is not a component element of the former. Consciousness is a synthetic unity of analytic data, but the data can exist only as correlated in the unity; and each datum, instead of being a component part of the unity, is the unity itself, viewed in some correlative aspect. A careful comparative study of conscious changes, and of the corresponding changes of the neurosis, gives ground for valid inferences

1. Bowne's "Introduction to Psychological Theory," p. 133.

concerning the classification of sensations. In this way, histology has helped to decide the question as to the existence of the muscular sense, and may yet throw more light upon the nature of the sense of innervation and the sense of the articular cartilages.

§3. *Metaphysical Assumptions.*—The physical stimulus of sensation, so long as it is characterized in terms denoting sensible objects, may properly be considered as a cause of sensation; but when so characterized, it is not antecedent to, or independent of, sensation. This leaves the causal agency, not without, but within, consciousness; that is, in *perceived* objects, the perception of which is always dependent upon sensation. When the physical stimulus is characterized in terms of atoms and molecular forces it passes beyond the range of sensibility, and hence beyond the scope of empirical science; and becomes metaphysical. To say that sensations are mechanically determined by physical stimuli, can have no possible meaning for empirical science except that one conscious state follows another in causal relations. While empirical science must stop here, no rational mind will or can do so. The nature of that which lies beyond the changing phenomena with which empirical science deals will and must be postulated, and such postulates are useful in guiding empirical researches. Such postulates, however, should not be confused with atoms and undulations, which are supposed to be actual components of *sensible* objects, but they should be recognized and acknowledged, and able to meet thorough criticism. The only postulate that can successfully meet such criticism is that of an infinite consciousness, regarded as the source of individual, or finite, conscious activity. All psychologists must admit that all objects of perception are products constructed in the perceptive process. To make any such product of perception, or any object inferred from an analysis of such product, the cause of the conscious activity that constructs or infers it, as every form of natural realism does, is to reverse the real order of facts. To make an acknowledged creation of consciousness the cause of the consciousness that creates it, is an absurdity; but to refer all finite consciousness to a correlative infinite consciousness as its source, is not only a logical, but a necessary conclusion; since finite consciousness, in all individuals, is in perfect harmony with the same *a priori* principles. This means that the real, which, in contrast with the ideal, is regarded as existing independently in quantitative relations of force, space, and time, is a strict correlative of the ideal; and hence, that both are essential factors of every state of finite consciousness. The discussion of this question will appear in the second book of this thesis.

BOOK II.

The Functions of Sensation and Intellection in the Cognition of the Real and the Ideal.

PART I.

CHAPTER I.

DISTINCTION BETWEEN THE REAL AND THE IDEAL.

This distinction rests upon the category of the absolute. Whatever is supposed to be absolute and unchangeable in itself is naturally regarded as existing independent of all finite consciousness, and is hence termed real, in distinction from the relative, or ideal, which is referred to finite consciousness as a causal agency. This distinction forms the basis of natural realism, which gives rise to metaphysics. Metaphysical reality is usually represented as transcending the range of all possible experience, yet as being an object of pure thought. The doctrine of metaphysical reality thus represents an object of thought, and consequently the act of consciousness by which it is apprehended, as entirely free from empirical or sensational conditions; and in so doing, violates the law of correlation. Infinite consciousness, of course, contains that which transcends the limitations of finite consciousness; but no object of finite consciousness, even though it may be called an object of pure thought, can be free from either of the correlative aspects of cognition, sensation and intellection. A metaphysical reality is thus a mere abstraction; since all possible objects of finite consciousness must present both aspects, the pure and the empirical.

The distinction between the real and the ideal, however, is necessary; and hence must rest on a universal process of thought, for only thus could it be clear or tenable. The ambiguity arising from this distinction, as made by different persons, comes from being carried too far. All agree in basing it upon the category of the absolute, some

L. of C.

include in it the category of substantiality, and still others include, in addition to this, the category of causality. Since only a relative distinction can be maintained, it would matter little, provided all persons were agreed, whether it was based one of the *a priori* categories or on more than one. For convenience of classification, the distinction, as made here, will rest on the category of the absolute; and the categories of substantiality and causality will be used to make subordinate distinctions in both the real and the ideal. The real, according to this distinction, is any object of consciousness viewed as absolute and unchangeable in itself; and the ideal is the same viewed as relative to the functions of consciousness.

As indicated in the classification of deductive concepts given on p. 54, both the self and the not-self of finite consciousness may be differentiated into the real and the ideal. The ideal self is further differentiated into the primary faculties of consciousness, viz., will, feeling, and thought. The real appears, when viewed under the category of activity, as force; when under the category of substantiality in the individual aspect, as mind; when in the universal aspect, as matter. The real is cognized in mathematical relations of force, space and time, according as it is referred respectively to the will, to thought, or to feeling. The ideal not-self becomes, when similarly referred to the will, to feeling, and to thought, the good, the beautiful, and the true. Finally the ideal-real, or infinite consciousness, although it must, in accordance with the law of mutual limitation, be regarded as in itself free from all finite qualification; must also, when viewed in correlation to finite consciousness, assume aspects corresponding to the primary functions of finite cognition.

According to the correlative distinction between the real and the ideal, the cognition of each is dependent upon the function of sensation as well as upon that of intellection. To make the truth of this statement evident the cognition of each must be analyzed.

CHAPTER II.

§1. *Cognition of Mind and Matter.*—Mind is cognized whenever any sense-object viewed under the category of substantiality assumes the individual aspect; when such object assumes the universal aspect, matter is cognized. Individuality of substance must not be confused with unity of substance or with indivisibility of substance. Spinoza's substance was a unity, but in it all individuality was lost. An atom is supposed to be an indivisible substance, but no individual characteristic is ascribed to an atom to distinguish it from other atoms of the same kind. Unity and indivisibility are both essential to individuality, but they do not constitute it. Individuality is that which distinguishes one indivisible unity from all others. Individuality of substance is cognized not in space, but in time. Substance, in time only, is mind, in space only, is matter. Mind and matter are thus correlative aspects of substance. When this correlation is overlooked, and the two are contrasted under the law of contradiction, it is quite natural for matter to assume the aspects of substance and causality, and for mind to assume the correlative aspects of phenomenon and effect. Materialism is thus a natural outgrowth of dualism. But substance, isolated from its correlate, phenomenon, is an abstraction; and matter and mind, when again isolated from each other, are but abstractions from abstractions. To cognize either mind or matter, one must regard some object under the category of substantiality, and emphasize, under the focus of attention, either the individual or the universal aspect of that substance. In

this act of cognition, both aspects of the object, substance and phenomenon, are involved, but the emphasis
must fall on the former.   To cognize either mind or matter thus requires all three of the primary functions of consciousness.   The will is represented by the movements of
attention; sensation is involved in the cognition of phenomena; and intellection, in the form of *a priori* categories, dominates the entire process.   ,

§2. *Cognition of Force.*—Force is one of the primary
phases of both the real self and the real not-self; and in
either case it may be viewed in relation to either the category of causality or the functions of the will.

The category of causality, when applied to physical
changes, assumes either the subjective aspect of effort or
the objective aspect of energy.   Effort and energy are
thus correlative aspects of force.   Either term implies the
other.   Effort is the intensive, energy the extensive measurement of force; that is, effort is the intensity of the feeling by which force is estimated, while energy is computed
in spatial and temporal terms.   There can be no effort
that is not put forth in time and space, nor can energy be
conceived except as the effort of some self as a center pull-
ing or pushing some not-self.

Force is thus cognized as a sensible object viewed under
the aspect of causality; and it is measured only in units
consisting of sense-objects which represent both the intensity of the effort and the relations of the energy to
space and time.   The unit of this measurement is the
horse-power, which is the elevation of 33,000 pounds one
foot in one minute.   To perceive this unit is to perceive
the pound weight, the foot of space, and the minute of
time.   The pound weight is the weight of about 28 cubic
inches of water.   In order to perceive this weight one
must lift the water and experience the effort required.   To
find its comparative weight by balancing it with a certain
volume of some other substance, gives no weight at all,
unless the weight of the latter substance be known by experience gained in lifting it.   This measurement of force is
an estimate of effort put forth in space and time.

Another way of measuring force is to find its equivalent in heat; but the measurement of this heat involves both subjective estimates of the feeling of temperature and objective measurement of time and space. In like manner, force may be measured by finding its equivalent in light or electricity; but the measurement of these, again, involves both subjective estimates of intensity of certain feelings and objective measurements of time and space.

Every method of measuring force thus involves both subjective estimates of intensity of feeling and objective measurements of time and space; and the subjective feeling must, in order to give any significance to the measurement of force, be that of effort. All other measurements are but comparisons based upon the horse-power. The sense of effort is essential to voluntary change. The intensity of the effort, or the effort as referred to the self, is the basis of all estimates of the strength of force as the cause of all change. The extensity of the effort, or the effort as differentiated and synthesized in *a priori* relations to the not-self, is the basis of all estimates of spatial magnitudes. The intensity of the effort rests upon muscular sensation. The extensity, as will be more evident after space-perception has been analyzed, rests upon tactual and retinal sensation.

The cognition of force thus involves the functions of will, feeling and thought. The will is involved in the objective form, volition; feeling, in the muscular and tacual sensations; and thought, in the *a priori* categories of quantity.

CHAPTER III.

§1. *Classification of theories*—Theories of space-perception do not necessarily depend upon the character assigned to space as metaphysical or empirical. All psychologists agree that all space-forms, as perceived, are products constructed in the act of perception. Dualists acknowledge that no extended data can enter the non-spatial mind to be elaborated and projected in space-form. Materialists acknowledge that the undulations transmitted to the brain centers cannot carry with them the forms or magnitudes of the objects perceived, also that such forms and magnitudes cannot be determined by the form, extent, or location of the brain-tracts stimulated. Dualists, materialists and idealists must all agree that all space-forms of consciousness are constructed in the act of perception, whatever the nature of that act may be.

A geometrical theory of space-perception was the only one ever definitely formulated before the time of Berkeley. This theory held space to be real and to be perceived by direct intuition in strict accord with the laws of the reflection and refraction of light. Various writers rejected this theory, but no definite hypothesis in opposition to it appeared, until Berkeley wrote his "Essay Toward a New Theory of Vision."

Attempts have been made to classify all theories of space-perception into two divisions, the "nativistic" and the "empirical;" but such a classification is not only defective but misleading. A theory may be both nativistic and empirical, as was Berkeley's. A complete classification must include three classes: One ascribing all original spatial data to purely sensational sources, or the Sensational Theory; another ascribing no spatial significance whatever to sensational functions, but attributing the origin of space-form to an intellectual process consisting of a reproductive association of successive, non-spatial, sensational data, or the Associational Theory; and a third, regarding space-form as a product of an intellectual synthesis, *a priori* and hence automatic, of all such sensational data as present the conditions essential to such synthesis, or the *A Priori* Synthetic Theory.

The sensational theory was first definitely formulated by Berkeley. It makes sensation the sole origin of all spatial data, from which, by processes of analysis and association, all spatial relations are developed. As advanced by Berkeley, this theory made no distinction between sensation and intellection, and hence failed to give any universal validity to spatial relations. The theory, somewhat modified in form, is still supported by prominent psychologists, especially by Dr. Ward and Prof. James.

The associational theory has many advocates among both the German and the English associational schools, the former being principally idealists, and the latter, realists. Lotze also must be classed among the supporters of the associational theory, notwithstanding the fact that his theory of "local signs" is pure sensationalism.

The *a priori* synthetic theory originated in Kant's distinction between the empirical and the *a priori* functions of consciousness; and, as Kant stated it, the emphasis was placed almost entirely upon the latter. The theory so modified as to place great emphasis upon sensational conditions, is ably supported by Prof. Wundt.

§2. Statement of the Three Theories.

(1.) *The Sensational Theory.*—BERKELEY states the principal points of this theory as follows: "But those lines and angles by means whereof some men pretend to explain the perception of distance, are themselves not at all perceived, nor are they in truth ever thought of by those unskillful in optics. I appeal to anyone's experi-

ence, whether, upon sight of an object, he computes its
distance by the bigness of the angle made by the meeting
of the two optic axes? or whether he ever thinks
of the greater or lesser divergency of the rays which
arrive from any point to his pupil? *   *   * Since,
therefore, those angles and lines are not themselves perceived by sight, it follows, from sect. 10, that the mind
does not by them judge of the distance of objects.
Secondly, the truth of this assertion will be yet further
evident to any one that considers those lines and angles
have no real existence in nature, being only an hypothesis
framed by the mathematicians, and by them introduced
into optics that they might treat of that science in
a geometrical way.   The *third* and last reason I shall
give for rejecting that doctrine, that though we should
grant the real existence of those optic angles, etc., and
that it was possible for the mind to perceive them,
yet these principles would not be found sufficient to explain the phenomena of distance, as shall be shown hereafter. *   *   * And, *first*, it is certain by experience, that
when we look at a near object with both eyes, according
as it approaches or recedes from us, we alter the disposition of our eyes, by lessening or widening the interval
between the pupils. This disposition or turn of the eyes
is attended with a sensation, which seems to me to be
that which in this case brings the idea of greater or lesser
distance into the mind. Not that there is any natural or
necessary connection between the sensation we perceive
by the turn of the eyes and greater or lesser distance.
But—because the mind has, by constant experience, found
the different sensations corresponding to the different
dispositions of the eyes to be attended each with a different degree of distance in the object—there has grown an
habitual or customary connection between those two
sorts of ideas; so that the mind no sooner perceives the
sensation arising from the different turn it gives the eyes.
in order to bring the pupils nearer or further asunder, but
it withal perceives the different idea of distance which

was wont to be connected with that sensation."[1] "*Secondly*,
an object placed at a certain distance from the eye,
to which the breadth of the pupil bears a considerable pro-
portion, being made to approach, is seen more confusedly.
And the nearer it is brought the more confused appearance
it makes. And, this being found constantly to be so, there
arises in the mind an habitual connexion between the
several degrees of confusion and distance; the greater
confusion still implying the lesser distance, and the lesser
confusion the greater distance of the object. This confused appearance of the object doth therefore seem to be
the medium whereby the mind judges distance."[2] "*Thirdly*,
an object being placed at the distance above specified, and
brought near to the eye, we may, nevertheless prevent, at
least for some time, the appearances growing more confused, by straining the eye. In which case, that sensation
supplies the place of confused vision, in aiding the mind to
judge of the distance of the object; it being esteemed so
much the nearer by how much the effort or straining
of the eye in order to distinct vision is greater."[3]

"In these and the like instances, the truth of the matter,
I find, stands thus: Having of a long time experienced
certain ideas perceivable by *touch*, as distance, tangible
figure, and solidity, to have been connected with certain
ideas of sight, I do, upon perceiving these ideas of sight,
forthwith conclude what tangible ideas are, by the wonted
ordinary course of nature, like to follow. Looking at an
object, I perceive a certain visible figure and colour, with
some degree of faintness and other circumstances, which,
from what I have formerly observed, determine me to
think that if I advance forward as many paces, miles, &c.,
I shall be affected with such and such ideas of touch, so
that, in truth and strictness of speech, I neither see distance itself, nor anything that I take to be at a distance.
I say, neither distance nor things placed at a distance are
themselves, or their ideas, truly perceived by sight."[4]

1 "Essay Toward a New Theory of Vision." Section 12-13.
2 id., Sections 21-2.
3 id., Section 27.
4 id. sec. 45.

DR. WARD supports the sensational theory in the following statements: "That space is a *priori* in the epistemo-
logical sense it is no concern of the psychologist either to
assert or to deny. Psychologically a *priori* or original in
such sense that it has been either actually or potentially
an element in all presentation from the very beginning it
certainly is not. * * We do not first experience a succession
of touches or of retinal excitations by means of movements, and then, when these impressions are simultaneously presented, regard them as extensive, because they
are associated with or symbolize the original series of
movements; but, before and apart from movement altogether, we experience that narrowness or extensity of impressions in which movements enable us to find positions,
and also to measure. But it will be objected, perhaps not
without impatience, that this amounts to the monstrous
absurdity of making the contents of consciousness extended. The edge of this objection will be best turned by ren-
dering the conception of extensity more precise. Thus,
suppose a postage stamp pasted on the back of the hand;
we have in consequence a certain sensation. If another be
added beside it, the new experience would not be ade-
quately described by merely saying that we have a greater
quantity of sensation, for intensity involves quantity, and
increased intensity is not what is meant. * * Attributing
this property of extensity to the presentation-continuum
as a whole, we may call the relation of any particular sensation to this larger whole its *local sign*, and can see that,
so long as the extensity of a presentation admits of
diminution without the presentation becoming nil,
such presentation has two or more local signs; its parts,
taken separately, though identical in quality and intensity, having a different relation to the whole. Such difference of relation must be regarded fundamentally as a
ground or possibility of distinctness of sign—whether as
being the ground or possibility of different complexes or
otherwise—rather than as being from the beginning such
an overt difference as the term 'local sign,' when used by
Lotze, is meant to imply. From this point of view we

may say that more partial presentations are concerned in the sensation caused by two stamps than in that caused by one. The fact that these partial presentations, though identical in quality and intensity, on the one hand are not wholly identical, and on the other are presented only as a quantity and not as a plurality, is explained by the distinctness along with the continuity of their local signs.'"[1]

PROF. JAMES supports the doctrine of "extensity" of sensations; but ascribes it, not to the presentation as a whole, but "to each and every sensation" of every sense. He states his own position as follows: "*Now, my first thesis is that this element, discernible in each and every sensation, though more developed in some than in others, is the original sensation of space*, out of which all the exact knowledge about space that we afterward come to have is woven by processes of discrimination, association and selection. 'Extensity,' as Mr. James Ward calls it, on this view, becomes an element in each sensation just as intensity is. The latter every one will admit to be a distinguishable though not separable ingredient of the sensible quality. In like manner extensity, being an entirely peculiar kind of feeling indescribable except in terms of itself, and inseparable in actual experience from some sensational quality which it must accompany, can itself receive no other name than that of *sensational element*. * * * It must now be noted that *the vastness hitherto spoken of is as great in one direction as in another.* Its dimensions are so vague that in it there is no question as yet of surface as opposed to depth; 'volume' being the best name for the sensation in question. *Sensations of different orders are roughly comparable, inter se, with respect to their volumes.*"[2]   "*In the sensations of hearing, touch, sight and pain we are accustomed to distinguish from among the other elements the element of voluminousness. We call the reverberations of a thunder storm more voluminous than the squeaking of a slate pencil.* * * * In the sensations of smell and taste this

---

1.   Ency. Brit., Vol. XX, pp. 53-4.
2.   James' "Principles of Psychology," vol. II, pp. 135-6.

element of varying vastness seems less prominent but not altogether absent."[1] "Now for the next step in our construction of real space: *How are the various sense-spaces added together into a consolidated and unitary continuum?* For they are, in man at all events, incoherent at the start."[2] "*How do we ARRANGE these at first chaotically given spaces into the one regular and orderly ' world of space' which we now know?*"[3] "Space *means* but the aggregate of all our possible sensations. There is no duplicate space known *aliunde*, or created by an 'epoch-making achievement' into which our sensations, originally spaceless, are dropped. They bring space and all its places to our intellect, and do not derive it thence."[4] "The essence of the Kantian contention is that there are not *spaces*, but *Space*—one infinite continuous *unit*—and that our knowledge of *this* cannot be a piece-meal sensational affair, produced by summation and abstraction. To which the obvious reply is that, if any known thing bears on its front the *appearance* of a piece-meal construction and abstraction, it is this very notion of the infinite unitary space of the world."[5] "Let no one be surprised at this notion of a space without order. There may be a space without order just as there may be an order without space. And the primitive perceptions of space are certainly of an unordered kind. The order which the spaces first perceived potentially include must, before being distinctly apprehended by the mind, be woven into those spaces by a rather complicated set of intellectual acts. The primordial largenesses which the sensations yield must be *measured and subdivided* by consciousness, and *added* together, before they can form by their synthesis what we know as the real space of the objective world. In these operations imagination, association, attention and selection play a decisive part; and although they no-

---

1 op. cit. p. 134.

2 id. p. 181.

3 id. p. 146.

4 id. p. 85.

5 id. p. 273.

where add any new material to the space-data of sense, they so shuffle and manipulate these data and hide present ones behind imagined ones that it is no wonder if some authors have gone so far as to think that the sense-data have no spatial worth at all, and that the intellect, since it makes the subdivisions, also gives the spatial quality to them out of resources of its own."[1] "*We seem thus to have accounted for all space-relations, and made them clear to our understanding. They are nothing but sensations of particular lines, particular angles, particular forms of transition or of particular out-standing portions of space after two figures have been superposed.*"[2]

(2.) *The Associational Theory.*—LOTZE's doctrine of "local signs," as before stated, is an inconsistent combination of hypotheses from both the associational and the sensational theories. The truth of this statement will appear from the following: "Many impressions exist conjointly in the soul, although not spatially side by side with one another; but they are merely together in the same way as the synchronous tones of a chord; that is to say, qualitatively different, but not side by side with, above or below, one another. Notwithstanding, the mental presentation of a spatial order must be produced again from these impressions. The question is, therefore, in the first place, to be raised: How in general does the soul come to apprehend these impressions, not in the form in which they actually are, —to-wit, non-spatial,—but as they are not, in a spatial juxtaposition? The satisfactory reason obviously cannot lie in the impressions themselves, but must lie solely in the nature of the soul in which they appear and upon which they themselves act simply as stimuli. On this account, it is customary to ascribe to the soul this tendency to form an intuition of space, as an original inborn capacity. * * * Let it be assumed that the soul once for all lies under the necessity of mentally presenting a certain manifold as in juxtaposition in space; How does it come to localize every individ-

1 op. cit. p. 143.

2 id. p. 152.

ual impression at a definite place in the space intuited by it, in such manner that the entire image thus intuited is similar to the external object which acted on the eye? Obviously, such a clue must lie in the impressions themselves. The simple quality of the sensation 'green' or 'red' does not, however, contain it; for every such color can in turn appear at every point in space, and on this account, does not, of itself, require always to be referred to the one definite point. Accordingly we conceive of this in the following way: Every impression of color r—for example, red—produces on all places of the retina, which it reaches, the same sensation of redness. In addition to this, however, it produces on each of these different places, a, b, c, a certain accessory impression, α, β, γ, which is independent of the nature of the color seen, and dependent merely on the nature of the place excited. This second local impression would therefore be associated with every impression of color, in such manner that $r \, \alpha$ signifies the same red in case it acts on the point a, $r \, \beta$ signifies the same red in case it acts on the point b. These associated accessory impressions would, accordingly, render for the soul the clue, by following which it transposes the same red, now to one, now to another spot, or simultaneously to different spots in the space intuited by it. In order, however, that this may take place in a methodical way, these accessory impressions must be completely different from the main impressions, the colors, and must not disturb the latter. They must be, however, not merely of the same kind among themselves, but wholly definite members of a series or a system of series; so that for every impression r there may be assigned, by the aid of this adjoined 'local sign,' not merely a particular, but a quite definite spot among all the rest of the impressions. The foregoing is the theory of 'Local Signs.' Their fundamental thought consists in this, that all spatial differences and relations among the impressions on the retina must be compensated for by corresponding non-spatial and merely intensive relations among the impressions which exist together without space-form in the soul; and that from them in reverse order there must arise, not a new actual arrangement of these impressions in extension, but only the mental presentation of such an arrangement in us."[1]

VOLKMANN formulates the associational theory from the idealistic stand-point, as follows: "Some of the more recent space-theories shift the basis of explanation of the space-form of the sensations of the muscles, pressure, and vision to those peculiarities of the senses which enable them to perceive simultaneously a multitude of series. We can, in this deduction, accept neither the premises nor the conclusion. From the mere simultaneity of sensations we cannot obtain the perception of a *side by side* arrangement, nor from mere succession that of a *one after another* relation. * * * If the sensations of pressure A and B are perceived as side by side simply because they are stimulated at the same time, then must the sounds A and B be perceived as side by side when the ear is struck by both waves of sound at the same time. * * * To distinguish two percepts as such has a double meaning, the negative one of their non-identity and the positive one of their duplicity or state of separation, or in short, of contrast and opposition. * * * The formation of spatial series takes place at a period which leads from that of the negative distinction into that of the positive. * * * Space form is by no means the prerogative of a certain class of sensations, but develops uniformly wherever the conditions for development are offered. * * * If after a sound series *a b c* the series *b a* follows, and our attention follows the sound qualities of the same, then the sound series *a b c* assumes the form of a space-series just as exactly as if the letters representing them signified colors, in which case, however, we do not claim the space to be that of the outer world. * * * Without doubt we conceive the scale thus formed as a real scale, i. e., as a space series in which the individual elements assume fixed positions. Where muscular sensations co-operate, as with the singer who sings the scale, or with the player upon the piano, then the production of space-form is specially favored. That

---

1 "Lotze's Outlines of Psychology,"Ladd's Tr., pp 50-53.

series of sounds but seldom rise to space-form is because the space-schemata of the sensations of the muscles, pressure, and vision are pre-eminently somatic and the scale can only be construed by an act of comparison. Furthermore, that the space-schemata of sounds is almost exclusively confined to the scale is easily explained, because outside the scale the return of the series in a reverse order depends entirely upon accidental circumstances, since it is seldom caused purposely, for by a reversal of the sound-succession the tune would be destroyed, or in other words, because musical symmetry is very different from that of architecture. The same may be stated about smells, only that, as the organ becomes very rapidly blunted, the distinct perception of successive and sufficiently strong sensations of odor deflects the perception from space-series into time-series."[1]

MR. HERBERT SPENCER supports the realistic form of the associational theory, as follows: "Extension under its several modes is cognizable through a wholly-internal co-ordination of impressions; a process in which the extended object has no share. Though the data through which its extension is known, are supplied by the object; yet, as those data are not the extension, and as until they are combined in thought the extension is unknown, it follows that extension is an attribute with which body does not impress us, but which we discover through certain of its other attributes."[2] "There is good reason to think, therefore, that the consciousness of space is reached through a process of evolution."[3] "All that can be reasonably inferred is, that these correlations and equivalences, mainly predetermined by the structure of the organism, are changed from their potential to their actual form by the experiences of the organism; and further that while the experiences disclose these latent connections between certain nervous actions and between certain correlative states of consciousness, they further the development

1 "Lehrbuch der Psychol." 3te Auflage, Bd. II, pp. 63-8.
2 "Principles of Psychology," Vol. II. p. 164.
3 id., p. 206.

of the structures and determine their details—serving at
the same time to give definiteness to their actions and to
the accompanying perceptions."[1] "Space, considered as
subjective, is derived by accumulated and consolidated
experiences from Space considered as objective."[2] "A solid
is decomposable into planes; a plane into lines; lines into
points; and as adjacent points cannot be conceived as distinct from each other, without being conceived as having
relative positions, it follows that every cognition of magnitude is a cognition of relations of position. * * Relations
of position are of two kinds: Those which subsist between subject and object; and those which subsist between
either different objects or different parts of the same object.
Of these the last are resolvable into the first. * * * All
relative positions may be decomposed into relative positions of subject and object. * * * These conclusions—
that Figure is resolvable into relative magnitudes; that
Magnitude is resolvable into relative positions; and that
all relative positions may finally be reduced to positions
of subject and object—will be fully confirmed on considering the processes by which the space-attributes of body
become known to a blind man."[3]

"We saw that our consciousness of Space is an abstract
of all relations among coexistent positions; that the germinal element of the consciousness is the relation between
two coexistent positions; that every relation between two
coexistent positions is resolvable into a relation of coexistent positions between the subject and the object touched;
that this relation of coexistent positions between subject
and object, is equivalent to the relation of coexistent positions between two parts of the body when adjusted by
the muscles to a particular altitude; and that thus the
question—How do we come by our cognition of Space? is
reducible to the question—How do we discover the relation of coexistent positions between two sentient points
on our surface?"[4] "The idea of space involves the idea of

1 op. cit., p. 170.
2 id. p. 182.
3 id., pp. 174-5.
4 id., p. 218.

coexistence, and the idea of coexistence involves the idea of space. * * * Two somethings cannot occupy absolutely the same position in space. And hence the coexistence implies space. * * * If now it should turn out that in the first stage of mental development a relation of coexistence is not directly cognizable, but is cognizable only by a duplex act of thought—only by a comparison of experiences, the theory of the transcendentalist will be finally disposed of. When it comes to be shown that the ultimate element into which the consciousness of space is decomposable—the relation of coexistence—can itself be gained only by experience; the utter untenableness of the Kantian doctrine will become manifest."[1] "It is the peculiarity alike of every tactual and visual series which enters into the genesis of these ideas, that not only does it admit of being transformed into a composite state in which the successive positions become simultaneous positions, *but it admits of being reversed.* The chain of states of consciousness A to Z, produced by the motion of the hand over an object, or of the eye along one of its edges, may with equal facility be gone through from Z to A. Unlike those states of consciousness constituting our perceptions of environing sequences, which do not admit of unresisted changes in the order of their components, those which constitute our perceptions of coexistences may have the order of their components inverted without effort— occur as readily in one direction as the other. And this is the especial experience by which the relation of coexistence is disclosed."[2]

(3.) *The A Priori Synthetic Theory.*—Kant stated the principal features of this theory, so far as he developed them, as follows: "Space is nothing but the form of the phenomena of all external senses; it is a subjective condition of our sensibility, without which no external intuition is possible for us. If then we consider that the receptivity of the subject, its capacity of being affected by objects, must necessarily precede all intuition of objects, we shall

1 op. cit., pp. 201-2.

2 id., p. 273.

understand how the form of all phenomena may be given before all real perceptions, may be, in fact, a *priori* in the soul, and may, as a pure intuition, by which all objects must be determined, contain, prior to all experience, principles regulating their relations. It is therefore from the human stand-point only that we can speak of space."[1] "Space and time are pure forms of our intuition, while sensation forms its matter. What we can know a *priori* before all real intuition, are the forms of space and time, which are therefore called pure intuition, while sensation is that which causes our knowledge to be called a *posteriori* knowledge, i. e., empirical intuition. Whatever our sensation may be, these forms are necessarily inherent in it, while sensations themselves may be of the most different character."[2] "Sensation, therefore, being that in the phenomena the apprehension of which does not form a successive synthesis progressing from parts to a complete representation, is without any extensive quantity. * * * Mere places or parts that might be given before space or time, could never be compounded into space or time."[3] "As the propositions of geometry are known synthetically a *priori*, and with apodictic certainty; I ask, whence do you take such propositions? and what does the understanding rely on in order to arrive at such absolutely necessary and universally valid truths? * * * If, therefore, space, and time also, were not pure forms of your intuition, which contains the a *priori* conditions under which alone things can become external objects to you, while without that subjective condition, they are nothing, you could not predicate anything of external objects a *priori* and synthetically. It is therefore beyond the reach of doubt, and not possible only or probable, that space and time, as the necessary conditions of all experience, external and internal, are purely subjective conditions of our intuition, and that, with reference to them, all things are phenomena

---

1 "Critique of Pure Reason," tr. by Max Mueller, p. 23.

2 id., pp. 37-8.

3 id., pp., 148-50.

only, and not things existing by themselves in such or such wise."[1]

WUNDT's statement of the *a priori* synthetic theory, as will appear from the following quotations, places great emphasis on the sensational conditions essential to the perception of space-form. "Concerning the perception of space we must draw from *a priori* principles the conclusion already reached by Leibniz and Kant, that space cannot, in objective reality beyond our consciousness, possess the form in which we see it. This conclusion follows from the stand-point now reached much more evidently than from the nativistic theory of space held by Kant. With an inborn form of perception which does not need to be developed, we might also regard it as a form which did not exist objectively and independent of our consciousness. However, nobody can imagine that reproductive and associative syntheses of impressions could exist outside of a reasoning consciousness. Here, therefore, remains no doubt that space, as well as time, in the form in which we perceive it, can exist only in our intuition. * * A single kind of isolated sensation never possesses this character, but wherever spatial objects are perceived, different sensation-complexes act together. * * Experience has also taught that the influence of motion becomes fixed so that the resting eye in measuring distances is influenced by the laws of motion. * * The necessity of a reproduction points to a psychological process mediating between the co-existence of sensations and the perception of space, and also establishes the fact that every spatially distinguishable point of the retina must be represented by a peculiar property of sensation possessed by it alone i. e., local colorization. * * Thus we reach that theory of space-perception which I call the theory of complex local signs, to distinguish it from other similar hypotheses of a more nativistic or empiristic tendency. This theory assumes two systems of local signs, whose relations to the eye may be represented as follows: The first system, the fixed local signs of the retina, forms in each eye a continuum of two dimensions. Of the second

op. cit., pp. 41-3.

system, which is connected with motion and which in the resting eye acts only as a reproducing factor, it is assumed that owing to the uniform condition and the intensive degrees of the sensations of space, it is a continuum of only one dimension. The process of space-perception we can briefly describe as a measuring of one manifoldly extended system of local signs of the retina by the uniform local signs of motion. As far as its psychological nature is concerned, this process is an associative synthesis; it is the union of both sensation-complexes into one product whose component elements can no longer be isolated in our perception. As these elements disappear entirely in the resulting product they are no longer separable in consciousness, which can perceive only the resulting product, space-form. There is a certain analogy between this psychical synthesis and a chemical synthesis, which from simple elements produces a compound which appears to our perception as a homogeneous whole with new properties. The general question that might be asked in regard to the latter can be answered at once by referring to the properties assigned to these two systems of local signs. Of both systems we can suppose that they are uniformly graduated, and thus that the most important property of space, graduation, is found in them. In addition, we find two other properties which distinguish space from time; the first is co-existence, the other, uniformity of directions. For the former property, the first system of local signs with its qualitative arrangement in two dimensions, analogous to the system of colors, forms the basis; the other is found in the second system, from which we can assume, on account of the merely intensive graduation possessed by it, that it forms for us the next motive to apply our ideas of measurement to space. In the organs of feeling, the relations seem to differ in so far that each individual part of the body in motion gives birth to a triple system of local signs, probably in consequence of the changing formation of folds in the skin produced by motion in different directions. We have also to recollect that in regard to local signs, as well as for space itself, the triplicity of measure-

ments depends entirely upon a mathematical form of construction, which rests upon the elements to be found, or
here upon the sign of a given locality."₁

§3.   CRITICISM OF THE THREE THEORIES:

(1.)   The Sensational Theory.—The sensational theory
fails thoroughly to analyze conscious phenomena, and
therefore, to show the presence and function of intellection
inp rimary stages of consciousness. Hence it bases the
validity of spatial relations, not upon a priori, but upon
sensational conditions. It assumes spatial sensations in
its premises, and so explains nothing as to the origin of
space-form.

Berkeley earned lasting fame by disproving the geometrical theory of space-perception, and establishing in its
place an empirical theory. The three data which he
named for estimating distance, ocular "sensations corresponding to" the angle of convergence, "confused appearance of the object," and the "straining of the eye" in ac-
commodation, are all factors of visual space-perception.
Berkeley's essay, however, is really concerned not so
much with the origin of space-perception, as with visual
estimates of spatial magnitude.

Dr. Ward's doctrine of the "extensity" of sensations
serves at best only to characterize, by a new name, space-
perception in its early stages; it gives no explanation at
all of its origin, His theory labors under two difficulties.
It reduces the earliest form of the presentation-continuum
to a pure sensation, and hence it must either make this an
extended sensation, or else deny that spatial relations enter into the earliest experiences. The first alternative is
to revert to Locke's sensational realism, the second is
virtually to abandon the sensational theory for the associational. Dr. Ward expressly repudiates the first, and
invents the doctrine of "extensity" to avoid the second;
but in order to do this successfully, two great difficulties
must be overcome. The extensity ascribed to sensation
must be void of all spatial magnitude, and the a priori

---

1 "Logik," vol. I. pp. 457-60.

validity of spatial relations must be established upon a sensational basis.

The doctrine of extensity, as illustrated by Dr. Ward, is based upon inferences from supposed cases which are absolutely impossible in actual experience; it represents experiences, which can come only from conscious states developed by both mental and physical activity, as carried back to a state supposed to precede all such activity. The "impression caused by a postage stamp pasted upon the back of the hand" would be much more significant to a consciousness in advanced stages of experience than to one in the earliest stages. What that impression is to the developed consciousness, is easily determined, and, of course, easily interpreted without resort to motion. But just what it would be in the first dawn of consciousness, and just how it would develop; in short, the whole problem of the origin of space-perception, is a question just as far from being answered as ever.

No consciousness whatever can exist "before and apart from movement altogether;" but even if it could, there would be no "massiveness or extensity of impressions in which movements enable us to find positions and also to measure." Extensity and positions are strict correlatives, and so are movement and measure. This doctrine of extensity thus separates strict correlatives and brings them into consciousness separately. If it should be so modified as to represent the presentation-continuum, in its earliest stages, as differentiated under *a priori* categories into analytic data which are simultaneously synthesized into space-form, thus involving not only sensation, but will, in the form of attention, and intellection in the form of spatial correlatives, then it becomes tenable; but it also ceases to be sensational and becomes *a priori* synthetic.

Prof. James explicitly declares that no absolute distinction can be made between sensation and intellection, and abscribes "all the categories of the understanding" to an "absolutely pure" sensation. As he uses the term, a sensation is a concrete object of consciousness; and

"*Sensations of different orders are roughly comparable inter se, with respect to their volumes.*" This doctrine of sensation would render it impossible to analyze processes of consciousness into their primary correlative factors, and would thus represent as a simple datum what is in reality complex. This brings Prof. James into conflict with Kant concerning the "piecemeal construction" of space, and with Prof. Ladd about the "eccentric projection" of sensations; but the disagreement comes not so much from difference of view as from difference of statement.

The "Kantian contention" is not "that there are not spaces," but that non-extended data cannot be summed together to produce extension. It has no bearing on the sensational theory; but it discloses the fundamental fallacy of the associational theory. Prof James is really in accord with this position of Kant's. Kant says, "Mere places or parts that might be given before space or time could never be compounded into space or time;" and James says of his "sensations," "They bring space and all its places to our intellect and do not derive it thence." James misunderstands and misrepresents Kant's view, confusing it with the associational theory. He asserts that in the Kantian view "there is a *quality produced* out of the inward resources of the mind, to envelop sensations, which, as given originally, are not spatial, but which, on being cast into the spatial form, become united and orderly."[1] This again describes, not the *a priori* synthetic theory, but the associational theory. The *a priori* synthetic theory, as Kant expressly declares, represents it as impossible for the sensations of the spatial series to be perceived at all without being synthesized into space-form.

Prof. Ladd's "epoch-making achievement" does not represent "sensations originally spaceless" as "dropped" into an empty intellectual space; but it represents sensational data and intellectual processes as simultaneously involved in the automatic analysis and synthesis of the presentation-continuum into space-form.

In order to explain the process of space-perception, it is

---

1 "Principles of Psychology," vol. II. p. 272.

necessary to make an absolute distinction between sensation and intellection, and to disclose the function of each
in the perceptive process. This Prof. James makes no attempt to do; but he continually confuses concrete objects
of sense with "absolutely pure" sensations, to which he
ascribes "vastness," "voluminousness" and "primordial
largenesses." The fundamental fallacy of Prof. James'
argument is the representation of consciousness as beginning in an undifferentiated state. No form of finite consciousness can exist that does not contain a self and a
not-self mutually related through functions of sensation,
intellection and volition. In the perception of space, as
well as in other forms of perception, these three functions
are simultaneously involved; and in an explanation of
space-perception, their character and mutual relations
must be disclosed. This, Prof. James makes no attempt
to do.

¶2. *The Associational Theory.*— The associational theory assumes the existence of successive, non-spatial sensations; and makes space-form a product arising from a
reproductive synthesis of these non-extended data. In
doing this, it necessarily commits one of two errors; it
must either start with non-spatial data in the premises
and end with only an assumed space in the conclusion; or
it must start with spatial data smuggled into its premises in such terms as "relations of position," "sensitive
surface," etc.

Lotze is one of the most inconsistent writers on space-
perception. As difficulties arise in the way of one theory
he abandons it for another, seemingly without being conscious of doing so, and so with the next; and thus he alter-
nately advocates and abandons both the associational and
the sensational theories. According to his premises, in which
he claims that all experience arises from non-spatial, sensational data, and to his method of deduction, which is by
means of a reproductive synthesis of successive, non-
spatial impressions, he must be classed as an association-
ist; but according to his doctrine of "local signs," the par-

ticular feature which has rendered his theory noted, he must be classed as a sensationalist.

Lotze's theory of sensation naturally leads him into confusion in the analysis of space-perception. Instead of a constantly changing presentation-continuum, he postulates a chaos of separate, non-spatial sensations in the soul, and hence finds it necessary for the soul "to apprehend these impressions not in the form in which they actually are—to-wit, non-spatial,—but as they are not, in a spatial juxtaposition." He states that the cause of this spatial grouping "cannot lie in the impressions themselves, but must lie solely in the nature of the soul." This is pure associationalism. Again, when the soul comes to localize every individual impression, "a clue must be in the impressions themselves." This, however, cannot be the simple quality of the sensation," but must be the "associated accessory impressions," by following which "the soul transposes the same red, now to one, now to another spot." This is pure sensationalism; and the two are in direct contradiction. Again, it would follow from the doctrine of "local signs" that each retinal element could see one and only one particular point in the objective "space intuited," and that the different retinal elements must be so arranged "that the entire image thus intuited is similar to the external object which acted on the eye." This is not only a fantastic form of sensational realism, making every point of an extended object imprint a corresponding spatial point upon the non-spatial mind; but it is contrary to facts of experience. So long as it is possible to see with a gradually diminishing retinal area, the vision is of the whole object growing less clear. Rays of light from all points of the object impinge upon certain retinal elements in or near the fovea, yet they are not intuited as coming from the same point in the object, as the theory of "local signs" represents. Lotze escapes from this difficulty, however, by abandoning the theory and appealing to the associations formed between retinal and motor sensations of the eye. This is a return to the associational theory, which, although it can do much to explain visual estimates of distance, can do nothing to explain the origin of space-perception. Lotze's doctrine is thus seen to be based upon fictions of the imagination, to contain irreconcilable contradictions, to misrepresent facts of experience, and to be based upon a sensationalism which would deprive spatial relations of all a priori validity.

Volkmann's distinction between the "contrast" and the "opposition," or the "non-identity" and the "duplicity" of percepts, may hold in a logical, but not in a chronological order. While the perception of non-identity is not the same as the perception of duplicity; neither perception can precede the other, hence it is meaningless to posit the origin of space-perception between the two, as Volkmann does.

In making all sensations assume a spatial order when they can be arranged in reversible series, he is compelled to ascribe to sounds, odors, and tastes, the quality of space-form; although he claims it to be not "the space of the external world." A space that is not the space of the external world is no space at all; but it is the only space that the associational theory can account for. Sounds, odors, and tastes must, in connection with their causal agencies, enter into spatial relations; but this does not mean that they form spatial series, or assume space-form. Volkmann is a good representative of that form of the associational theory which starts without spatial data in the premises and ends without space-form in the conclusion.

Mr. Spencer's theory is the reverse of Volkmann's. It starts with spatial data involved in the terms applied to the perceiving subject, and the only spatial relations accounted for are those assumed in the subjective organism. It is really not an explanation of the origin of space-perception, but a theory of the evolution of an extended organism conscious of its own extension. Mr. Spencer derives "space considered as subjective" from "space considered as objective;" and in doing so, he performs a feat as remarkable as it is impossible. He divides a solid into non-extended points, which he arranges into "relations of

position;" and then makes the perception of these relations of position the origin of the perception of space. He
makes the "germinal element" of space-perception "the
relation between two co-existent positions" which "is resolvable into a relation of co-existent positions between
subject and object touched." Hence, "the question—How
do we come by our cognition of space? is reducible to the
question—How do we discover the relation of co-existing
positions between two sentient points on our surface?"
The only logical result of this argument which reduces the
origin of space-perception to the consciousness of "a relation of co-existent positions between subject and object
touched, * * * between two sentient points on our
surface," is to identify one of the "two sentient points on
our surface" with the perceiving subject, and the other
with the "object touched." This is a form of natural
realism, more realistic than Locke's; for it need not go below the "sentient points on our surface" while Locke's
had to reach the tablet of the mind.

Mr. Spencer is right in making the "germinal element"
of the perception of space the process by which "we discover the relation of coexisting positions between * * *
points on our surface;" but he is wrong in limiting the
number of the points to two, in making them sentient, and
in representing the consciousness of our surface as preceding, in any way, the consciousness of the mutual relations
of its parts. The consciousness of our surface is the consciousness of the relations of its parts; it originates in and
develops with a consciousness of such parts, not merely of
two, but of all of them, so far and so fast as they are
differentiated in consciousness.

Mr. Spencer mistakes again in supposing that "the idea
of co-existence involves the idea of space." Sounds, odors,
and tastes may be co-existent, and may be perceived to be
so; yet Mr. Spencer himself says "No one will allege that
sound, as an affection of consciousness, has any space-attributes."[1] In making a relation of co-existence "cogniz
able only by a duplex act of thought," he implies that it is

---

[1] "Principles of Psychology," Vol. II, p. 181.

possible for an act of thought to be absolutely simple. This error seems to lie at the root of all forms of natural realism, and it has been sufficiently discussed already in the definition of sensation. Co-existence and succession are strict correlatives in every act of thought; and hence Mr. Spencer, in deriving a consciousness of co-existence from a reversible series of successive percepts, commits the fallacy of bringing strict correlatives into consciousness singly.

In describing spatial percepts as forming a series in which the successive order can be varied more freely than it can in a series of non-spatial percepts, Mr. Spencer inverts the real facts in the case. Sounds can be arranged in a series, the successive order of which can be not only reversed, but varied at will; but every series of spatial percepts is limited to a fixed order of succession, the only possible variation of which is an exact reversal. This fixed serial order is the fundamental characteristic of sensational data involved in space-form.

The only space accounted for by Mr. Spencer is that assumed in the conditions ascribed to the perceiving subject. When, by "a process of evolution," "correlations and equivalences mainly pre-determined by the structure of the organism are changed from their potential to their actual form by the experience of the organism," it is plain that the "structure of the organism" is already spatial, and that the "correlations and equivalences" are as "actual" in "their potential" form as in any other; but it is not quite so clear just what is the subject of the "experience of the organism," unless it be the "sentient points on our suface." It is plain, however, that Mr. Spencer's analysis of space-perception, when carried to its logical outcome, reduces to an exaggerated form of natural realism, which represents the perceiving subject as extended in space and as perceiving its own space-form.

(3.) *The A Priori Synthetic Theory.*—Kant outlined the fundamental principles of this theory, which may be stated as follows:—The universal validity of spatial relations must rest upon an *a priori* basis; space cannot orig-

inate from an association of successive, non-spatial data;
both sensation and intellection are essential to the perception of space; space-form is a product arising from a synthesis, *a priori*, and hence automatic and instantaneous,
of all sensational data that present the conditions essential to such synthesis.   In the main, Kant correctly set
forth these principles, although not so clearly as might be
wished.   Two marked peculiarities of his philosophy confused not only his statements, but his own views as well.
His radical dualism, appearing in his antitheses of pure
and practical reason, sense and understanding, pure and
empirical sensibility, concepts of understanding and ideas
of reason, and phenomena and noumena, necessarily dis-
torted his view of the character and relations of the functions of consciousness.   Again, the special emphasis
which he laid on the intellect made him appear to represent space as existing in a pure form of thought previous
to all sensation.   In spite of the confusion of his views
and statements, however, it seems evident that he meant
to represent this pure form of space as merely a fundamental process of thought, and to make both sensation
and intellection essential and simultaneous functions of
space-perception.

Prof. Wundt accepts Kant's doctrine of space, founds
it upon a basis both sensational and intellectual, and ascribes to space perception both an origin and a development in experience.   He corrects Lotze's doctrine of "local
signs" by making it necessary for sensations to be sharply
differentiated qualitatively in order to be localized in space-
form.   Wundt is right in ascribing to sensations an acquired tendency to suggest associated sensations of another kind, and in making this tendency an important
factor in developed space-perception; but the importance
of this factor lies in its use in estimating spatial magnitudes, not in orginating space-form as he supposes.   This
error is doubtless responsible for the fallacy of the advocates of the associational theory—they fail to discriminate
between the origin of space-form and the estimate of its
dimensions after it has been perceived.   The processes are

not entirely separate; yet, in explaining space-perception, there must be an absolute distinction between the two. One is automatic and instantaneous, the other develops in experience; hence, while Wundt is right in positing a synthesis of sensational data as mediating between the perception of such data and the perception of space-form, it is a productive synthesis, *a priori* and instantaneous, as Kant stated, and not a reproductive synthesis as held by Wundt.

As Wundt maintains, this synthesis is of a mathematical nature, similar to a synthesis of geometric coördinates; but his scheme of making a continuum of one dimension of muscular sensation, with which to measure the retinal continuum to which he ascribes two dimensions, is not only highly imaginary but really absurd. A spatial continuum of only one dimension, or of only two, is a mere abstraction having no possible meaning, except as referred to a continuum having all three dimensions. Besides, the idea of measuring one sensational continuum by another is misleading. There can be but one presentation-continuum, which, when it becomes spatial, must assume all three dimensions at once. Spatial estimates of the presentation-continuum are all based on tactual perception; so-called measurements resulting from visual estimates always refer to corresponding tactual experience.

In passing from a geometric synthesis of sensations to their fusion into a new compound, Wundt commits a gross error. A sensational continuum may be differentiated into analytic data, and each datum held in a synthesis; but their fusion into a new compound means their annihilation, and a sudden transition to an entirely different continuum, a continuum rapidly fading from consciousness. Prof. Wundt's treatment of space-perception is very suggestive, and does more to explain the problem than any other cited above; but it involves untenable assumptions which must be eliminated before it can be accepted.

§4. RELATIONS OF THE MENTAL FUNCTIONS.

(*1.*) *The Will.*—Both forms of this function are promiinent in the perception of space. Spatial distance is but a limitation to the effort of a finite consciousness, and effort involves volition; hence volition is essential to the idea of distance. Again, spatial position implies serial order, and serial order involves movement of attention; hence attention is essential to the idea of position. From this it follows that the experiences in which the sense of effort is greatest, give emphasis and fixedness to spatial distances, while experiences in which it is least, give great freedom to movements of attention, and a corresponding facility to the discrimination of positions.

No one can doubt the above statement concerning the attention; but some doubt might be felt concerning the dependence of the sense of effort upon volition, on account of the distinction which psychologists make between active and passive effort. When the muscles are stimulated artificially, the resulting affections are rightly enough termed, by way of contrast, passive sensations of effort; but if in this experience there were no associations recalling volition, as the natural cause of such affections, they would have no meaning as sensations of effort. Unless differences of sensational quality discriminated under the movements of attention were ascribed to corresponding volitions as causes, there could be no spatial distance between them, and hence they would be separated, not in space, but in time.

(2.) *Feeling.*—Since subjective feeling is a correlative of objective, both forms must be involved in space-perception; but objective feeling, or sensation, is much the more conspicuous. Only in the sense of weariness does subjective feeling become prominent, in which form it influences the estimates of distance. Sensation is essential both to the estimate of distance and to the discrimination of positions. Only as referred in causal relation to effort, can sensation give rise to distance; and only as voluntarily differentiated into qualitative contrasts, which sustain fixed mutual relations, can it give rise to positions. Only muscular and tactual sensations are inseparably connected with the sense of effort, and hence, with the perception of space. In addition to these, only retinal sensations can be varied in exact correspondence with voluntary changes in the sense of effort; and hence, only the percepts of the muscular, the tactual, and the retinal senses can assume space-form. All other percepts assume spatial relations in connection with their causal agencies; but instead of appearing as things occupying space, they seem to be only the effects of the percepts of the muscular, the tactual and the retinal senses, which percepts appear as things occupying space.

The dependence of spatial order upon voluntary changes in the sense of effort, can be illustrated by comparing a sensational continuum of eight tactual percepts with one of the eight tones of the scale. The successive order in the latter can be varied so as to pass through each tone in direct or reverse order, through only each alternate tone, or through them in any order whatsoever. The successive order in tactual percepts is fixed, so that the only possible variation is an exact reversal. In sound, one can choose his starting-point, direction, successive order, and stopping-place; but in tactual and retinal perception, the successive order is fixed. The cause of this fixed order lies in the exact correspondence of all voluntary changes in tactual and retinal sensation to the accompanying voluntary changes in the sense of effort.

The muscular sense, since it is essential to all sense of effort, must be regarded as fundamentally involved in the perception of space. The tactual also, since it is inseparably connected with voluntary muscular sensation, must be regarded as similarly involved. The retinal sense, as before stated, cannot be so regarded. It is not essential to the sense of effort, and besides, people blind from birth have acquired considerable knowledge of space. But since all voluntary changes in retinal sensation are involved in a fixed serial order of relations, corresponding exactly to that of the changes of effort associated with them as their causes, and since the sense of effort connected with them is comparatively insignificant, it becomes the most efficient sense for discriminating spatial positions; and, when guided by tactual associations, an efficient means for estimating distances also.

(*3.*) *Intellection.*—The *a priori* analysis and synthesis involved in space-perception consists in an automatic differentiation of the presentation-continuum into the correlative contrasts, vertical and horizontal, the former of which assumes the correlative aspects, up and down, while the latter is again differentiated into the correlative contrasts lateral and longitudinal, the former assuming the correlative aspects, right and left, and the latter those of back and forth. Being strictly correlative, these three pairs of aspects must simultaneously appear in the presentation-continuum, hence the analysis and synthesis are simultaneous. The presentation-continuum thus becomes spatial, not through a piece-meal process of reproductive association; but through an *a priori* process, automatic and instantaneous, in which the correlatives, position and magnitude, motion and measure, up and down, right and left, back and forth, all originate and develop together.

Only as referred to voluntary changes in the sense of effort, have these correlative terms any meaning; only as connected with qualitative changes in sensation, can they be perceived; and only as held in an intellectual synthesis preserving all their mutual relations, can they give rise to space-form. These three functions of consciousness, volition, sensation, and intellection, characterize all stages of finite consciousness. Intellection is identical in all perceiving subjects, and thus gives to spatial relations their *a priori* validity; sensation varies in each subject, and thus occasions the variations of individual perspective. To base local significance upon sensational quality annuls all universal validity of spatial relations; but to base it upon an intellectual synthesis of an invariable order of relations which qualitative changes of sensation sustain to the movements of attention, makes the validity of spatial relations universal. The sensational differences are necessary, for no intellectual synthesis of relations can exist unless supported by sensational differences. Hence to fuse sensational differences into a new compound, as Wundt's theory does, destroys both the analytic data and the synthetic continuum at once.

That space-form is a product arising from an intellectual synthesis of the relations which sensational data sustain to volition, is evident from the following facts. Sounds, odors, and tastes, in which the successive order of qualitative changes does not vary in conformity to changes of effort, do not assume space-form; but are regarded as merely subjective affections caused by tactual or visual percepts. In visual perception, where the sense of effort is reduced to a minimum, all estimates of distance rest upon tactual associations. Visual space-form is regarded as real only as it represents tactual conditions; and it varies automatically in strict accord with all variations, real or supposed, in such conditions. Variations can be voluntarily introduced into visual space-form, corresponding to changes merely supposed in tactual conditions. Thus a concave surface can be made to appear convex, and conversely. The same set of geometrical lines can be made to assume different forms corresponding to objects viewed from different directions. The principles of perspective rest entirely upon the tendency to interpret visual perception as merely representative of tactual. This tendency becomes so strong that it cannot be entirely overcome. Students of free-hand drawing have great difficulty in estimating it properly, and in representing objects as they would appear if projected on a plane surface. Great errors in the estimates of forms and distances in visual perception result from misinterpreting the tactual conditions involved; but when such inferences are corrected, the errors in spatial estimates disappear.

Again, in tactual perception, when the serial order of successive percepts is abnormally changed, the perception of spatial relations is correspondingly changed. It even becomes necessary, in such cases, to correct one's inferences from present tactual conditions by comparing tactual perception with visual, and by coördinating the results of the two. Prof. James well illustrates this with facts which he quotes from well-known cases of anaesthe-

sia. His own words are as follows:—"We get such results
as are given in the following account by Professor A.
Strümpell of his wonderful anæsthetic boy, whose only
sources of feeling were the right eye and the left ear; * *
* * 'He had no feelings of muscular fatigue. If, with
his eyes shut, we told him to raise his arm and to keep it
up, he did so without trouble. After one or two minutes,
however, the arm began to tremble and sink without his
being aware of it. He asserted still his ability to keep it
up. Passively holding still his fingers did not affect him.
He thought constantly that he opened and shut his hand,
whereas it was really fixed.'"[1]   In speaking of another
case, Prof. James continues, "Or we read of cases like
this: 'Voluntary movements cannot be estimated the
moment the patient ceases to take note of them by his
eyes, if one asks him to move one of his limbs either
wholly or in part, he does it but cannot tell whether the
effected movement is large or small, strong or weak, or
even if it has taken place at all. And when he opens his
eyes after moving his leg from right to left, for example,
he declares that he had a very inexact notion of the extent of the movement.'"[2]   In explaining such facts, Prof.
James makes the following significant remarks: "It is,
in fact, easy to see that, just as where the chain of
movements is automatic, each later movement of the chain
has to be discharged by the impression which the next
earlier one makes in being executed, so also, where the
chain is voluntary, we need to know at each movement
just *where we are in it*, if we are to will intelligently what
the next link shall be. A man with no feeling of his movements might lead off never so well, and yet be sure to get
lost soon and go astray. But patients like those described,
who get no kinæsthetic impressions, can still be guided by
the sense of sight. Thus Strümpell says of his boy: 'One
could always observe how his eye was directed first to the
object held before him, then to his own arm; and how it
never ceased to follow the latter during its entire move-

1 "Principles of Psychology," Vol. II. pp. 489-90.
2 id. p. 490.

ment. All his voluntary movements took place under the unremitting lead of the eye, which, as an indispensable guide, was never untrue to its functions.' * * * I have myself reproduced a similar condition in two hypnotic subjects, whose arm and hand were made anæsthetic without being paralyzed. They could write their names when looking, but not when their eyes were closed."[1]

The construction of space-form, including both the magnitude of distances and the location of positions, is thus seen to be an intellectual process, in tactual perception, as well as in visual; and space-perception is also seen to require, in order to become much developed, a co-ordinating comparison of the two. The tactual gives fixedness of distance, the visual, facility in the discrimination of positions; both combined, give a highly developed perception of space. The only element of space-perception that is fixed and unchangable is the intellectual synthesis of the mutual relations among the sensational data. The intensive force, or voluntary effort, is changeable; the sensational data are in constant change; every object in space is constantly changing its position, in relation not only to the consciousness of the individual subject, but also to other objects as they are related in universal consciousness. The head and feet, right hand and left, back and face, as bases of spatial relations, differ in each perceiving subject; and in the experience of all conscious subjects alike, the north star, even, is constantly changing position in relation to other objects in space. This intellectual synthesis, being fixed and absolutely unchangeable, may be called real; and the sensational data, being in relative change, may, in correlation to it, be called ideal. Not that one is independent of consciousness and the other a mere conscious affection; but that the one is absolutely unchangeable in all perceiving subjects alike, and the other constantly changing in relation to each individual subject. Thus, only as fixed in conscious processes are spatial relations unchangeable. Up and down, right and left, back and forth, all represent fixed aspects, not in the objective

---

1 op. cit. pp. 490-92.

world, but in conscious processes. They cannot originate in generalizations from the sense-world, for they are the basis of the construction of the sense-world. They cannot come from an abstraction of the three dimensions of space, for the three dimensions of space rest upon them. Before mathematicians can prove the existence of a fourth dimension of space, they must disclose a fourth correlative contrast in the *a priori* differentiation of the presentation-continuum, on which to base it. This is not only impossible, but the idea seems illogical. The three correlative contrasts are *a priori* in all forms of finite consciousness, so far as known, both in human beings and in lower animals. It is logical to suppose that in all forms of finite consciousness they are essentially *a priori*, and that, in all alike, they give rise to an intellectual synthesis of sensational data into space-form.

CHAPTER IV.

PERCEPTION OF TIME.

§1. *Number of Theories.*—Only two theories have been definitely formulated to explain the nature of the perception of time. One of these theories regards time as a metaphysical reality independent of consciousness, and holds that it is perceived as a flux because it flows along in consciousness. This theory has been very appropriately termed by Dr. Nichols, who has given its latest and fullest statement, the "process theory." The other theory is indifferent to the character of time in itself, but holds that as it is perceived it is a product resulting from an instantaneous intellectual synthesis of relations among sensational data. This theory is now supported by many psychologists, but since it was originated by Kant, in connection with his theory of space, and since it is in some respects very similar to that theory, it seems very appropriate to call it the synthetic theory.

§2. STATEMENT OF THE TWO THEORIES.

(*1.*) *The Process Theory*—Dr. Nichols states the principal points of this theory as follows: "But we must not fail to note that these changes are not the only components of these ideas, and that these image processions, and also their prototype original processions, are not all change; there must be duration without change in order for duration with change to be possible."[1] "But according to this, one thing above all else must be carefully noted, *perception*, or perception of time-duration is *always a process and never a state.; a certain definite time is a certain definite process.*"[2] "The classic question, therefore,

---

1 "Psychology of Time," p. 130.

2 id., p. 113.

whether the idea of succession is or is not a succession of
ideas, in so far as the question is one as to whether the
idea is a longitudinally passing *process*, or a sidewise presented *state*, may as well be fought out with reference to
the nature of any original sensation and for the briefest
temporal portion of it, as with reference to any train
or series of such sensations."[1] "And it is plain also that
we have in such an idea no such occurrence as that
described by Herbart, or Mr. Ward, or any of those who
conceive that an idea of a series, or of a succession, or of
time, must be some sort of instantaneously painted picture presenting the whole length of time or of the series in
a simultaneous perspective. * * * We do not '*now*' perceive this something, whatever it is, but so far as I can discover we 'now-now-now-now' perceive it; we do not
stand still and look along the line to measure this past in
a perspective view, but *run* along the line as it were to
measure it inch by inch, or present by present, by a moving process."[2] "We are inclined to conclude therefore
* * * that the duration of the sensation or series,
the perception of the duration, and the perception of the
length of the duration are one and identical; that the duration is an ultimate datum, and no more capable or need-
ful of other explanation or of further analysis than the blue-
ness of the blue spot."[3] "Sensations and their images or
reproductions have various attributes; qualitatively they
are blue, or warm, or painful, etc., intensively they are
strong or weak, bright or faint, etc. Duration, or continuation, is another attribute or characteristic of every
sensation and of every image. This attribute is the ultimate and essential datum of time."[4] "*We must, with*
GREATEST *care distinguish between perceiving time and
apperceiving time relation* * * * Without some qualitative or some intensive *change* there can be no temporal
relation."[5] "Thus if we supposed a creature to be so

---

1 op,. cit. p. 117.

2 id. p. 117-18.

3 id., p. 119.

4 id., p. 113.

5 id., pp. 120-21.

simple as to be without memory, and capable from time
to time of but a single elementary sensation of constant
quality, say of pain, (such perhaps are some infusoria)
we should say that pain was *perceived* whenever it occurred; we should not say it was *apperceived.* We should
also say that such a creature *perceived* time."[1] " But how
do we *measure* time length, and measure ' how *long* ago '
and 'how long until'? When speaking of our simple creature capable of but a single constant sensation, we said
that when his pain lasted five seconds, he perceived the
length of five seconds, and when it lasted one second, he
perceived the length of one second.   We distinctly de-
clared he did not apperceive either length, and from what
we have said of change and relations it is clear that I have
not conceived that this creature perceived relations of any
kind; neither relations of difference nor of numbers."[2]

(2.)   *The Synthetic Theory.*—Kant expressed his views
of time as follows:—"Time is not an empirical concept deduced from any experience, for neither co-existence nor
succession would enter into our perception, if the representation of time were not given *a priori.*   Only when
this representation *a priori* is given, can we imagine that
certain things happen at the same time or at different
times.   * * *   On this *a priori* necessity depends also the
possibility of apodictic principles of the relations of time,
or of axioms of time in general.   * * *   To say that
time is infinite means no more than that every definite
quantity of time is possible only by limitation of one
time which forms the foundation of all times.   The original representation of time must therefore be given as unlimited.   * * *. Time is nothing but the form of the internal sense, that is, of our intuition of ourselves, and of
our internal state.   Time cannot be a determination peculiar to external phenomena.   * * *   Time is therefore
simply a subjective condition of our intuition (which is
always sensuous, that is so far as we are affected by ob-

---

1 op. cit., p. 114.

2 id. pp. 128-9.

jects), but by itself, apart from the subject, nothing."[1]

Prof. Bowne supports the synthetic theory, as follows: "However real time may be, the subjective origin of the notion will be the same as in the ideal theory; and however ideal time may be as an existence, its actual function in our mental life will be unchanged."[2] "There is nothing to do but to declare that the time idea rests ultimately upon an original and peculiar mental principle, whereby it connects its experiences under the special form of sequence. * * * All the conceptions which enter into a perception of sequence co-exist in one form or another in the present consciousness. That which constitutes their temporal order is not any existing succession, but the peculiar form of their relation within the field of consciousness. Hence the act of consciousness by which relations of sequence are grasped must itself be without any temporal distinctions in itself; and in this sense the consciousness of time is non-temporal."[3] "No inspection of consciousness will reveal to us the origin of this idea, inasmuch as the idea is always there long before the reflective consciousness begins the inquiry. We can only study some of its logical conditions."[4]

Prof. Höffding supports this theory, and makes some valuable statements concerning the measurement of time. "Change, transition, alternation and inner-connection throughout all change—these were the most important characteristics of consciousness. But in these the form of time is already given. Psychology must therefore come to a pause at this form, as something originally given, a psychological ultimate presupposed in all conscious phenomena, which cannot be itself made an object of explanation. It is different when the question is of the *idea* of time, of temporal relations. This idea has its psychological history like every other. * * * The idea of time involves therefore two things: (1), *the consciousness of*

1 "Critique of Pure Reason," Max Mueller's Tr., pp. 27-30.
2 "Introduction to Psychological Theory," p. 128.
3 id. p. 130.
4 id. p. 128.

change, of succession; this arises through contrast to a constant sensation; (2), repetition of certain states which have a strong hold upon consciousness; the *recognition* of these makes a certain measuring and grouping possible in the series of changes.

"It would not be possible, from a simple constant sensation or a simple constant feeling, to have the idea of time. The more we are absorbed in a single thought, the more we are 'rapt,' as it were, out of time; for which reason the mystics call eternity an 'enduring present.' On the other hand, the idea of time could not possibly be derived from mere succession of sensations; something would be needed that might lead to the surveying and measuring of the succession. * * * * So long as the idea of time is grounded only on the change of our inner states, the estimation of time is very uncertain. Two circumstances are in this connection of especially great importance; the interest in the content of the experience and the number of traits experienced. The interest in what is experienced may have very diverse influence. In concentrating the attention and so preventing consciousness from noticing the succession, it shortens the time both during the actual experience and in the remembrance. Seven years passed for Jacob like a few days, because he loved Rachel. But interest may also lengthen the time, since we involuntarily argue from the importance and significance of the content that a long time must have elapsed. * * * Each individual brings his own scale of measurement, depending in part on the more or less energetic interest with which he spends his life and attends to the passing events, in part on the speed with which his ideas are accustomed to move. * * * The need of substituting an objective scale of measurement for the subjective, the uncertainty of which must easily have been noticeable, made itself early felt. * * * We measure by the help of uniform movements in nature. But this uniformity has itself to be established, so that we move here in a circle. Absolute time might be thought as realized in nature, so long as it was believed with Aristotle that the heavenly bodies revolve with eternal immutability and uniformity; but, this belief once abandoned, the idea of absolutely uniform time loses its basis in reality. * * * An absolutely uniform time is an ideal, requiring that every possible estimation of time shall be subjected to a further correction. Every standard which has been tried with a view to absolute uniformity, has proved to be variable. Only in the symbolical representation of time as a line is absolute uniformity to be found. But here idealizing abstraction has put its hand to the work. The conception of absolute time is a mathematical abstraction.",[1]

Dr. Ward gives the following discussion of the synthesis involved in the perception of time: "Granting this implication of simultaneity and succession, we may, if we represent succession as a line, represent simultaneity as a second line at right angles to the first; empty time—or time-length without time-breadth, we may say—is a mere abstraction. Now it is with the former line that we have to do in treating time as it is, and with the latter in treating of our intuition of time, where, just as in a perspective representation of distance, we are confined to lines in a plane at right angles to the actual line of depth. * * * * This truism —or paradox—that all we know of succession is but an interpretation of what is really simultaneous or coexistent, we may then concisely express by saying that we are aware of time only through time-perspective, and experience shows that it is a long step from a succession of presentations to such presentation of succession. The first condition is that we should have represented together presentations that were in the first instance attended to successively, and this we have both in the persistence of primary memory images and in the simultaneous reproduction of larger or shorter portions of the memory-train. In a series thus secured there may be time-marks, though no time, and by these marks the series must be distinguished from other simultaneous series. To ask which is first among a number of simultaneous presentations is unmeaning; one might be logically prior to another, but in

1 "Outlines of Psychology," Eng. Tr., pp. 184-90.

time they are together and priority is excluded. Nevertheless after each distinct representation a, b, c, d there probably follows, as we have supposed, some trace of that
movement of attention of which we are aware in passing
from one presentation to another. In our present remin-
iscences we have, it must be allowed, little direct proof of
this interposition, though there is strong indirect evidence
of it in the tendency of the flow to follow the order in
which the presentations were first attended to. With the
movements themselves we are familiar enough, though
the residua of such movements are not ordinarily conspicuous. These residua, then, are our temporal signs, and,
together with the representations connected by them, constitute the memory-continuum. But temporal signs alone
will not furnish all the pictorial exactness of the time-perspective. They give us only a fixed series; but the working
of obliviscence, by insuring a progressive variation in intensity and distinctness as we pass from one member of
the series to the other, yields the effect which we call time-
distance. By themselves such variations would leave us
liable to confound more vivid representations in the distance with fainter ones nearer the present, but from this
mistake the temporal signs save us; and, as a matter of
fact, where the memory-train is imperfect such mistakes
continually occur. * * * But, though the fixation of
attention does of course really occupy time, it is probably
not in the first instance perceived as time, i. e., as continuous 'protensity,' to use a term of Hamilton's, but as intensity. Thus, if this supposition be true, there is an
element in our concrete time-perceptions which has no
place in our abstract conception of time. In time conceived as physical there is no trace of intensity; in time
psychically experienced duration is primarily an intensive
magnitude, witness the comparison of times when we are
'bored' with others when we are amused. * * * We are
absorbed in the present without being unwillingly confined to it; not only is there no motive for retrospect or
expectation, but there is no feeling that the present endures.
Each impression lasts as long as it is interesting, but does

not continue to monopolize the focus of consciousness till attention to it is fatiguing, because uninteresting. In such facts, then, we seem to have proof that our perception of duration rests ultimately upon quasi-motor objects of varying intensity, the duration of which we do not directly experience as duration at all. They do endure and their intensity is a function of their duration; but the intensity is all that we directly perceive."[1]

§3. CRITICISM OF THE TWO THEORIES.

(1). *The Process Theory.*— This theory is based upon an erroneous view of the nature of change. On the one hand it holds to the existence of time as an infinite flux previous to all change, as a necessary precondition of change; on the other, it holds to the existence of a finite consciousness in which change does not appear. An infinite process previous to, or independent of, change, is a contradiction in terms. A consciousness in which change does not appear is an infinite consciousness. This double error in the fundamental principles of the process theory necessarily leads it into numerous inconsistencies. It represents a "simple creature capable of but a single constant sensation" as perceiving a "process," as perceiving "the length of five seconds;" hence, since "we do not *now* perceive" time, but "'now-now-now-now' perceive it," since we "*run* along the line as it were to measure it inch by inch," this "simple creature" would have to "run along the line to measure it inch by inch" while experiencing "but a single constant sensation." Again, since this creature can not "perceive relations of any kind," the time which it perceives can contain no relations and hence must be an "attribute or character of every sensation." But this reduces time to a sensational or subjective phenomenon, instead of an objective reality existing before all conscious changes. In disputing the synthetic view, Dr. Nichols very frankly admits that the question, as to whether the perception of time is an instantaneous act or a successive process, can be settled just as well with refer-

ence to the shortest perceptible interval as to any period
however long. This, however, if the process theory is to
hold good, involves the infinite divisibility of sensible
time, since, according to this theory, the shortest perceptible time is a process which, in turn, must be composed of
shorter periods, each of which is again a process, and so
on *ad infinitum*. The only escape from this difficulty is
the abandonment of the process theory; and Dr. Nichols,
when he says, "We do not *now*, but 'now-now-now-now'
perceive" time, does virtually exchange it for the theory
of unconscious units of consciousness. One "now" gives
no conscious "present," but four of these unconscious
nows summed together give one conscious "*now*," which
can be used to measure time "inch by inch, or present by
present." If this "inch, or present," as its name implies,
be in the "present" consciousness, and it must be if it is
used as a measure, then the process theory is abandoned
for that of unconscious units of consciousness. But if
this "inch, or present," be not all in the present consciousness, if it be a succession of shorter periods each of which
is a conscious process of successive periods still shorter,
and so on *ad infinitum*, then sensible time must be infinitely
divisible. But if sensible time were infinitely divisible, no interval, however short, could elapse. For instance, let one second be the interval. It is evident that
before the last half of the second can arrive the first half
must have elapsed. But since it cannot go all at once
the first half of it must have elapsed before the second
half can arrive. And since no extent of time, however
short, can elapse all at once, it would be necessary for an
infinite process of division to reduce the interval to absolute zero before it could elapse. But no infinite process of
division can reduce extension to absolute zeros; consequently sensible time cannot elapse in any such process.
The only possible way in which it can appear in consciousness is as an instantaneous perspective in which the correlative aspects, before and after, appear together and
give time-form. The advocates of the process theory,
overlooking the correlative nature of these terms, which

are essential to time-form, represent them as entering consciousness separately, which is impossible.

(2). *The Synthetic Theory.*—Kant disclosed the facts
that time can be perceived only in connection with change,
and conversely, that change cannot be perceived without
assuming time-form; also that time-perspective cannot be
a piece-meal construction, but that it is an instantaneous
product resulting from an automatic, intellectual synthesis. Kant makes no attempt, however, to explain the
nature of the intellectual synthesis which gives rise to
time-form.

Prof. Bowne shows that, whatever may be the nature
of time in itself, sensible time "rests ultimately upon the
original and peculiar mental principle, whereby it connects
its experience under the special form of sequence," and
that "the act of consciousness by which the relations of
sequence are grasped must itself be without temporal distinction." But instead of attempting to explain the
nature of this non-temporal act, he declares such explanation beyond the reach of rational attempts.

Prof. Höffding agrees that the origin of time-form is "a
psychological ultimate presupposed in all conscious phenomena, which cannot itself be made an object of explanation." He claims, however, that "It is different when
the question is of the *idea* of time, of temporal relations,"
and claims that "This idea has its psychological history
like every other."

Both of these writers, have done much to render the
nature of time-perception clear to the student of psychology, and yet both have, according to their own statements, attempted the impossible, when they rendered
this service. Prof. Bowne makes it absurd to explain
even the idea of time. Prof. Höffding makes "time-
form" a subject before which psychology must "come to a
pause," but grants to "the *idea* of time" the possibility
of an analysis. The fact is that the only subjects before
which psychological analysis must "come to a pause" are
arbitrary creations of imagination; moreover if any
problems lie hopelessly beyond the reach of such investiga-

tion, they lie in ultimate facts of individual consciousness rather than in any such facts of universal consciousness as the perception of time. And when Prof. Bowne described the "act of consciousness by which the relations of sequence are grasped" he analyzed the conditions of the origin of the "idea" of time. Prof. Höffding, also, when he discussed the "psychological history" of "the *idea* of time," was at the same time investigating into the conditions and origin of "the form of time;" and in doing so he has enumerated facts connected with the estimates of duration that are very significant, and which will be referred to later.

Dr. Ward, without any limitations of subject, or any distinctions between the form and the idea of time, proceeds to give one of the best analyses ever given of the conditions and processes involved in the perception of time. But from the fact that he makes no distinction between time-form, as original in all perception, and the developed idea of time resulting from reflection and abstraction, there is sometimes a possible ambiguity in his statements, as, for example, when he says that "in a series thus secured there may be time-marks, though no time." This might be construed as meaning that time-form is a product of experience; but a construction that seems more in harmony with the writer's position would make it refer, not to an individual consciousness in which time-perspective had not yet appeared, but to certain facts of consciousness which enter into but do not constitute the perception of time. This ambiguity of statement, together with an undue emphasis given to the intensity of sensation as determining the estimates of duration, and a corresponding failure to properly emphasize the functions of weariness in the same respect, constitute the principal defects in Dr. Ward's excellent analysis of time-perception.

§3. MENTAL FUNCTIONS.

(1). *The Will.*—The function of attention in time-perception, as in space-perception, is to discriminate position in the order of relations. Volition proper, including effort, does not directly influence time-perspective; but indirectly, through desire, interest, and weariness, it is the chief factor in determining temporal distance. The feeling of weariness, in connection with interest and desire, greatly increases distances in time-perspective. It is not the intensity of sensation that increases this distance, as Dr. Ward supposed; for when no weariness is felt, both interest and intensity of sensation tend to make us unconscious of duration. Prof. Höffding noted the different effects of interest upon apparent duration, but attributed the difference to the importance attached to the object of interest, and argued that greater importance in the object gives greater time-distance. His illustration, however, argues against his theory; for to Jacob, Rachel was a most important object of interest, and yet, as Prof. Höffding admits, "Seven years passed for Jacob like a few days." But if Jacob was like other mortals, the years of waiting must have seemed longer to him when he was weary than at other times. Temporal distances may be estimated intellectually by a comparison of objective changes; but such estimate is meaningless unless it is referred to time-perspective, as determined by interest qualified by weariness.

(2). *Feeling.*—In feeling also, the subjective form is prominent in the perception of time. Feelings of pain of any kind, but especially of weariness, give greater distance in time; while feelings of pleasure tend to make anyone unconscious of duration. Sensation is necessary, since without it there could be no consciousness; but quality of sensation has nothing to do with the flow of time, except as it gives rise to feelings of pleasure or of pain. As a means of estimating duration, however, recurrence of similar sensations is necessary; since temporal distance, like spatial, can be measured only by repeating a constant unit of measurement.

(3). *Intellection.*—The intellectual synthesis is much simpler in time-perspective than in spatial. Instead of three correlative contrasts in the sensational continuum, only one appears, that of before and after. This, together with the categories of identity and change, and coëxistence and succession, must enter every possible stage of finite consciousness, and must automatically give rise to the construction of time-form, in which, as an instantaneous present, both past and future must appear simultaneously and inseparably. Many more empirical elements enter into developed stages of consciousness than into primitive stages; but in every possible stage, consciousness is differentiated by *a priori* categories, one of which is that of before and after; hence there can be no stage of perception that is not characterized in its time-perspective by both memory and expectation.

Both distance and position, in the perspective of both memory and expectation, are largely dependent upon intellectual processes. When the thoughts are absorbed in the object, the present hardly seems to endure; but when they turn frequently to self, time seems to lengthen. When the ordinary course of thought is disturbed, subjective displacement of temporal order occurs. Who has not, sometimes, after having failed to understand words when spoken, yet, upon subsequently and accidently discovering the thought of the speaker, heard distinctly the words spoken and located them in the time-perspective, not in the order understood, but as they were spoken? Why should not the vague impression upon the ear be carried forward to the time when it received meaning instead of the meaning being carried back to the vague sounds? Apparently because the category of causality determined the position in the time-perspective, and hence it corresponded to the position of the causal agency. In memory the category of causality governs, to a great extent, position in the time-perspective.

As stated and illustrated by Prof. Höffding, all subjective estimates of duration must be corrected by objective comparison; and for such correction, no invariable objective standard exists. Every possible perception of time involves both aspects, the subjective, the relative, the ideal, and the objective, the absolute, the real; and in every estimate of duration, whether subjective or objective, reference must be made in some way, directly or indirectly, to changes in spatial relations. No change can occur in either time or space that does not involve a corresponding change in the other. Time and space are thus strict correlatives, the former referring all changes to the self as subjective, and the latter referring them to the not-self as objective. As consciousness becomes absorbed in the not-self, time-perspective gives way to space-perspective; and changes are regarded not so much in their successive relations in time as in their causal relations in space. When consciousness objectifies the self, time-perspective becomes prominent. The self, in contrast with the not-self, appears as relative, ideal, finite, and the not-self assumes the opposite aspects, absolute, real, infinite; yet, since these aspects are strictly correlative, both classes of contrasts are, as has been shown, essential to the perception of both space and time. Space, in contrast with time, appears stationary, while time appears as an endless flux; yet, when either space or time is objectified in contrast with the perceiving subject, it becomes an infinite continuum, in which the perceiving subject changes, and through which it passes; and conversely, when the perceiving subject is objectified it becomes a fixed identity before which the changes of both space and time continually pass in an endless process. Should the perceiving subject "run along the line," as represented in the process theory, time would be a fixed continuum; only when the subject is fixed can time be a process. And in the perception of the flux of time, just as in the perception of motion in space, the *from which* and the *to which*, the *before* and the *after*, must appear simultaneously. It is as faulty to represent the subject as being conscious or unconscious *in* time, as *in* space. He may be unconscious of certain temporal as well as of certain spatial relations; but he is not conscious or unconsciousness *in* either, except in so far as his feelings may be said to change in time.

The statement made on p. 100 that force, space, and time are correlative phases of the real, as it is referred respectively to the will, to thought and to feeling, can now be made more clear. Will and force are corresponding phases of the ideal self and the real self, when viewed under the category of causality. Just as the motive phase of consciousness, or the will, is a correlate of the sentient phase which presents both aspects, thought and feeling; so the causal phase of the real self, or force, is a correlate of the substantial phase, which presents both forms, space and time. In the same way that thought and feeling are correlatives, the one being objective and fixed, and the other subjective and changeable; space and time prove correlatives, the one being objective and fixed, and the other subjective and changeable. Thus the parallelism is complete, showing that the three fundamental phases of the real, force, space, and time, rest upon the three fundamental phases of consciousness, will, thought, and feeling; and since the latter are essential functions of all finite consciousness, the former are correlative phases of all objects of finite consciousness. Not that all such objects must assume the aspects of energy, or of space-form, or of time-form; but that they must, in entering into finite consciousness, become related in some way to force, to space, and to time.

PART II.

Cognition of the Ideal

CHAPTER I.

The Good, the Beautiful and the True.

§1. The Good.

(1). *Definition.*—The good has already been referred to as the phase of the ideal not-self dependent upon motivity. This does not mean that it is not also a phase of the self; nor could it so mean, since the self and the not-self have been recognized as correlatives. But inasmuch as the good, the beautiful and the true, when objectified, become a not-self opposed to the perceiving self, it is proper to define them as the ideal phases of the not-self in correlation to the fundamental phases of the conscious self, will, feeling, and thought respectively.

Every object of consciousness involves change, change emphasizes the causal phase of the ideal, or volition, volition implies motive, motives are good or evil; hence the perception of any object of consciousness may, if the attention be so directed, give rise to the cognition of the good. All people discriminate between good and evil motives, howevermuch they may differ as to the nature of the distinction. This universal fact must rest upon a psychological basis that is universal; and, at the same time, the individual differences in the distinction, as made by different persons, show that such psychological basis must include individual as well as universal characteristics. A reference to the tabulation of deductive concepts on p. 54 will show that such is the case, and that the distinction of the good, the beautiful and the true, from their opposites, the evil, the ugly and the false, does, in each case, rest upon such basis; also that the individual characteristics are most predominant in the case of the beautiful, and least in that of the true. From this it follows that the only universal distinction that can be made in regard to either the good, the beautiful or the true is a general one, which must be further defined by each individual as he applies it to specific objects.

The only definition of the good that has universal validity is, that motives are good in so far as they subordinate the interests of the individual self to universal interests, and evil in so far as they subordinate universal interests to the interests of the individual self. When it is necessary to decide what particular acts meet the requirements of the good, individual differences must appear; but since strictly individual differences can not be defined, a further definition would not be universally valid. But although the good cannot be further defined, it can be differentiated into two correlative forms, the subjective or conscience, and the objective or duty.

(2). *Conscience.*—Conscience is the subjective feeling of obligation that arises in the cognition of the good as connected with one's own volition, and that impels one to act accordingly. This feeling cannot be educated in the strict sense of the term, but education can greatly develop it. Education deals with processes of thought; but thoughts awaken corresponding feelings, hence a proper education will strengthen conscience. Conscience thus exists in very different degrees of force. With some it is authoritative, with others it is only persuasive, and with still others it is merely impulsive. This last form of conscience is fundamental and universal. All the finer types are evolutions from it.

(3). *Duty* is the definite conception of such volition as will result in good. In its general form, it is concisely expressed in Kant's *categorical imperative,* "*Act in con formity with that maxim, and that maxim only, which you can at the same time will to be a universal law.*"[1]

1 Watson's "Selections from Kant," p. 241.

In particular cases, duty must be defined from the standpoint of individual conditions, and such conditions continually vary. A great evil frequently resulting from stereotyped definitions and rules of duty is the reduction of conduct to mere formalism. A similar evil comes from an injudicious bestowal of rewards and punishments, which cheat the one on whom they are bestowed out of the natural fruit of goodness of character. Goodness consists in a sacrifice of individual interests to universal interests, not in a sacrifice of one individual interest to another. The reward of fidelity to duty is strength of character, which gives both subjective satisfaction and objective advantages. Any artificial reward is a species of wages, which transfers conduct from the sphere of duty to that of hired service. But, on the other hand, duty does not consist in a mere sacrifice of one's wishes to the wishes of another, unless such sacrifice promotes universal interests; and no universal rule for determining what will promote general welfare can be given.

(4). *Mental Functions.*—The most prominent of the mental functions in the cognition of the good is will in its objective form, volition. Feeling is emphasized in its subjective form in conscience; and intellection lays special emphasis upon the categories of self and not-self, individuality and universality, cause and effect, and activity and passivity. These categories are all involved in every act of duty, for every such act requires the individual self to do or to suffer in order to promote the universal interests of both the self and the not-self.

§ 2. THE BEAUTIFUL.

(1). *Definition.*—Beauty is that quality of all objects of consciousness the cognition of which is conducive to universal pleasure. At first thought, this definition may seem too broad, since there are connected with universal pleasure certain feelings that seem to pertain solely to the lower animal nature. The contemplation of animal or physical comfort is usually regarded as the opposite of the contemplation of representations of the beautiful; but when this comfort is conducive to universal pleasure, its representation and contemplation involve the cognition of the beautiful. Many rare works of art, both of painting and of poetry, picture to the aesthetic imagination the enjoyment of just such comfort; and the only requirement of such productions is that they represent this comfort as being conducive to universal pleasure.   It is a great stroke of genius to represent in suggestive imagery pleasures of this kind, which have become sacred to the memory through cherished associations.   Another apparent criticism upon the definition of beauty given above is that in many works of art pronounced beautiful, there is much that is conducive to universal pain.   In all such works of art, if there were not other elements that were still more conducive to universal pleasure, they would cease to be works of art and become relics of barbarism.   The only distinction between works of art and such relics of barbarism is the test found in the definition of the beautiful given above.   So long as they are universally pleasing, they are works of art; when a different culture renders them repulsive, they become relics of barbarism.   Every finite work of art thus contains the ugly as well as the beautiful.

The elements of goodness and truth form essential elements of the beautiful.   When a work of art represents bravery and self-sacrifice, although it must be conducive to pain in every beholder, still it yields a pure type of pleasure that is universal.   Evidences of design, also, yield an exquisite pleasure to all admirers of nature, to devotees of science as well as of art.   In the beautiful as well as in the good, there are two forms, the subjective, or aesthetic taste, and the objective, or art.

(2). *Aesthetic Taste.*—This bears the same relation to art that conscience does to duty.   It rests upon the sensibility, it is the ideal factor, the element that impels to expression.   Aesthetic taste is a birth-right; no amount of experience or culture could originate it.   Education may develop it, just as it does conscience, but the capacity must be inborn; and the most exquisite forms of it, represented by the finest art, are but evolutions from the primordial germ that finds expression in the tattooing or the war-paint of the savage.

(3). *Art.*—Art is the objective realization of the beautiful. It is the embodiment of the beautiful in concrete objects which conform to universal laws of aesthetic taste. It is a philosophical classification that distinguishes between fine arts and useful arts; but the distinction rests, as will be seen later, upon the relative freedom with which all qualitative changes in the sensations of the different senses can be voluntarily controlled, rather than upon lack of utility, on the one hand, or the absence of beauty, on the other. The subject-matter of many gems of fine art is the representation of certain forms of the useful arts; and, on the contrary, many products of the useful arts involve a combination of fine arts. To the true artist, there is beauty in every product of honest toil. If there were no beauty in the real facts when

" The mug of cider simmered low,
The apples sputtered in a row,"

then there would be no beauty in " Snow Bound." The chief beauty, both in the real facts and in the artistic representation of them, lies in the cherished associations of memory; and the commemoration of these associations is the great object of fine art. To accomplish this the artist struggles for that freedom of expression which is found only in connection with the associations of sight and hearing. In both of these senses there are general rules for the synthesis of individual elements into universal unities, giving symmetry of form and harmony of sounds and colors. The fine arts representing the associations of sight are architecture, sculpture, and painting; those representing the associations of hearing are music, poetry and oratory. But in all these arts, where freedom of expression and general rules for order are found, there remain many individual variations subject to no law except that they must be universally pleasing. Invariable symmetry and constant harmony become tiresome. Some of the finest effects of music, as for example, the minor key, come from blending sounds whose wave lengths interfere. The ideal element is always prominent in art. It is that which brings reality in all its freshness directly to consciousness. As in the good so in the beautiful, the ideal and the real elements are not only essential, but correlative.

(4). *Mental Functions.*—In a comparison of the mental functions involved in the cognition of the beautiful, the will appears least prominent. It enters only indirectly. The attention is always involved in the cognitive process, and in addition to this, volition becomes an indirect factor in the subject-matter of all representations of moral action.

Feeling, both subjective and objective, appears most prominent, the former in aesthetic taste, and the latter in the subject-matter of all works of art. Subjective feelings might be classified as sensational, moral and intellectual, according as they arise principally from sensation, or from the contemplation of motives or of designs. Objective feelings might be classified as emotional, including auditory and visual sensations, and as sensual, including all other sensations.

Intellection appears in all rules for symmetry, rhythm, and harmony.

§3. THE TRUE.

(1). *Definition.*—The true is cognized when any object of consciousness discloses a system of relations which synthesizes individual data in one universal whole. In so far as finite cognition represents all individual data as harmonized in one all-inclusive system of relations, it is true; but in so far as it fails to do so and represents them as in discord, it is false.

In the *real*, individual data are synthesized and related to the conscious self in terms of force, space and time; but in the *ideal*, the self and the not-self are synthesized in an order of relations which harmonize individual characteristics in universal concord, and which correlates all finite selves in an infinite self.

(2). *Judgment.*—The subjective form of the true, or

judgment, is the consciousness of individual data as subsumed by means of an all-inclusive system of relations in
one harmonious whole.   In the *real* the judgment deals
with questions of *fact;* in the *ideal*, with questions of
right, or *fitness*.   The judgment is the faculty which, in
the fullest sense of the term, can be educated; yet it can
not be created by education.   It must exist before there
can be anything to educate.   Its psychological basis,
which is the consciousness of unity in plurality, is universal.

(3).   *Plan.*—The objective form of the true, or *plan*, in
the *real*, rests on universal processes of thought expressed
in relations of force, space, and time.   In the *ideal*, plan
involves universal processes of thought, but its distinctive
feature is its variability relative to each individual self in
its correlation with the universal self, or relative to each
finite self in its correlation with the infinite self.

(4).   *Mental Functions.*—In addition to attention,
which is essential to all cognition, volition appears both
in the purpose of the plan and in the self-subordination of
the individual to the universal.

Subjective feeling appears in the sense of harmony, objective feeling in the sensations involved in the sense of
harmony.

Intellection lays special stress upon the categories of
self and not-self, individuality and universality, cause and
effect, activity and passivity, and the absolute and the relative.   These categories, of course, are not at first consciously present, that is, are not objectified under the attention in the cognition of the true; but they unconsciously
dominate the cognitive processes from the beginning, and
when this process is developed and made an object of attention, their nature and function become manifest.   Especially is this the case with the category of the absolute
and the relative, which underlies the distinction between
the real and the ideal.   As in the cognition of the real, so
in that of the ideal, both the absolute and the relative are
essential factors; but while in the cognition of the real the
former is emphasized, in the cognition of the ideal, on the

other hand, the latter is emphasized. Thus the laws according to which all relations of force, space and time are synthesized are universal, unchangeable, absolute; but the laws according to which all relations of goodness, beauty and truth are synthesized must vary in relation to each individual. This places the two spheres in contrast, as the absolute and the relative, or, the real and the ideal. But since the contrast, not only between the absolute and the relative, but between the antithetic terms of each category, is strictly correlative; so must the contrast between the real and the ideal be correlative. In uniting these correlative aspects of consciousness, cognition is compelled to contemplate that which transcends all finite limitations, and which, since it must appear to finite cognition both as real, and as ideal, may be appropriately termed the *ideal-real*.

CHAPTER II.

§1. *Definition.*—The ideal-real "that` shall satisfy the facts and truths to which both Realism and Idealism appeal" is the infinite consciousness which, as a correlate of finite, changeable consciousness, is not subject to change. In so far as the self changes in accordance with invariable laws, it is a universal self; in so far as it changes in accordance with no law but its own, it is an individual self; in so far as it changes at all, it is a finite self; but in so far as it does not change at all, it is an infinite self. Since change and identity are *a priori* correlates characterizing finite consciousness, every conscious self is both finite and infinite; also, the finite self is both individual and universal. The contrast between the finite self and the infinite self is thus a contrast, not between a self and a not-self, but between a limited self and an unlimited self. The finite self exists in the infinite self. There is no individual self incommunicable to the infinite self, since the finite self is known only to and through the infinite self. In the infinite self, conscience, aesthetic taste and the sense of right have absolute authority; change and its limitations of force, space and time are here transcended; and goodness, beauty and truth are eternal.

§2. *Mental Functions.*—In passing from finitude to infinitude, the limitations of finite thought must necessarily be reflected in all possible representations of the infinite; hence all *a priori* categories applied to the infinite must be subject to the law of mutual limitation. The category of substantiality represents the infinite self as unchangeable; and that of casuality, as an agent acting in time and space. The difficulty here is that the *a priori* categories come into conflict when finitude attempts to comprehend infinitude. The only rational procedure is to recognize the source of the conflict as lying in the limitations of finite cognition, and to realize that the only way in which a unity can appear to such cognition is through pairs of correlative aspects. In the same way that the conflicting aspects of the finite self are harmonized in a synthesis of correlative opposites, so must the conflicting aspects of the infinite self be correlated; and just as the synthesis is subject to the law of mutual limitation governing the application of the *a priori* categories to the finite self, so also must it be in their application to the infinite self. The apparent conflict lies, not in the nature of the infinite, but in the limitations of finite cognition, which reflects its own limitations on all its objects.

From the stand-point of the will, the cosmological argument has represented the infinite as the first cause; and from the same stand-point, Christian theology holds to the incarnation of the Word.

From the stand-point of feeling, the faith argument has represented the infinite as revealed through a direct intuition of feeling; and from the same stand-point, Christian theology holds to the individual manifestation of the Holy Spirit as a personal Comforter.

From the stand-point of intellection, the teleological argument has represented the infinite as the designer of the universe; and from the same stand-point, Christian theology holds to the omniscience of the Father Almighty.

Each of these representations, like the psychological function on which it rests, if taken separately, reduces to a mere abstraction; but if taken in correlation, the three representations lead to a concrete intuition of the infinite. This trinity, then, instead of being three separate beings, is the finite representation of the three correlative phases of the one Being which, in comprehending the individuality of every finite self, is ideal; in being absolute and unchangeable, is real; and in being thus both ideal and real, is infinite, the infinite Self. And since every finite self is a correlate of this infinite self, it is necessarily finite, not as an individual, isolated in space and time, but as an eternal element in the concrete being of the "Ideal-Real."

·